MASALA
FARM

MASALA FARM

Stories and Recipes from an
Uncommon Life in the Country

by Suvir Saran

with Raquel Pelzel and Charlie Burd

Photographs by Ben Fink

CHRONICLE BOOKS
SAN FRANCISCO

LIBRARY OF CONGRESS CATALOGING-IN-PUBLICATION DATA AVAILABLE.
ISBN 978-0-8118-7233-1

MANUFACTURED IN CHINA

DESIGNED BY JACOB T. GARDNER
TYPESETTING BY DC TYPOGRAPHY, SAN FRANCISCO

10 9 8 7 6 5 4 3 2 1

CHRONICLE BOOKS LLC
680 SECOND STREET
SAN FRANCISCO, CALIFORNIA 94107
WWW.CHRONICLEBOOKS.COM

Dedication

There are a number of beings—human and animal—to whom I dedicate this book.

To Nana (my maternal grandfather, Chaman Lal Bhardwaj) and Michael Batterberry, two grand men, who lived separated by seas and continents but who lived lives quite similar in the brilliance of their content, the richness of their thoughts, and the ideas and inspiration that they left behind for countless many. My most supportive and loving influencers, I wish you new chapters of your lives and souls that are just as rich, or richer still. How blessed I am to have been gifted by your presence.

To Karun Deep Sagar, my nephew, who I hope will continue to enrich and better this grand world that Nana and Michael have left behind. Your destiny I shall never see, but I know it will be full of riches, some waiting to be discovered, others better because you have already found them. The farm is as much yours as ours. Enjoy it for what it is, a symbol of life everlasting.

To Charlie, Seema, and Ajit—three pillars of strength that I have had on my side, always. Charlie, thanks for your constant and epic partnership. Thanks also for always having my life organized so that I can keep sharing and learning every day from my travels through this land and others. Seema and Ajit, thanks for being siblings and elders—all at once. I am blessed, what more can I say?

To Kali, beloved cat of many memorable years, who never allowed a moment to pass without making her presence known, and to Simba, who deeply mourned Kali's passing but consoled us with his acute desire to cuddle and hug. Kali, you were the ultimate gourmand who enjoyed Battenkill Valley Creamery milk every bit as much as we do. No other milk was ever good enough.

To the blue heron that was here, picking a fish from the pond every time we came to see the house before we bought it—an early omen for me that this was the farm we wanted. We are lucky she comes back daily. And to all the other lives, big and small, that inhabit the farm today, and shall tomorrow: This farm is more yours than it is ours. Your presence makes us feel blessed. Your joy is ours doubled. Your safety our mission. May you always prosper and keep our home and lives enriched by your presence.

TABLE *of* CONTENTS

❀

✻

CHAPTER FOUR: WINTER

FOREWORD

Because I am a baker, most people assume that sweet things are my passion. In truth, though I love to bake, I've always favored the flavor of spice. I was captivated by Indian cuisine more than thirty years ago during a month-long visit to India. It was not in restaurants, however, where I found the best food; it was in the home of friends who had a gifted chef. Mealtime was the highlight of every day, and it was never the same twice. I learned that Indian food isn't just about fire and spice; in the hands of a skilled cook, as well as being brilliantly vibrant, it can be a kaleidoscope of complexity, balance, and subtlety. By the end of my stay, it seemed that most other food was bland and uninteresting by comparison.

I longed to return to India, not just for the food but also for the exquisite beauty of colors and crafts and the extraordinary warmth of the people. I never expected to encounter all of this right in my own hometown until I met Suvir Saran when I interviewed him for a *Food Arts* magazine story on sugar. Michael Batterberry, founding editor, suggested that since we are both contributing editors, I should speak to Suvir about the unrefined Indian sugar called jaggery. After our first conversation, we became fast friends; many years later, Michael Batterberry wrote forewords for both of our cookbooks—the only ones he ever offered—creating a deeper priceless bond. Suvir expresses it as being siblings, and indeed we are; I think of us as kindred spirit twins: sugar and spice!

We have many other things in common in addition to food, such as our big-city beginnings that metamorphosed into a devotion to nature, a deep connection to the land, and an appreciation for country living. In gravitating to the rural countryside of Hebron, situated in a verdant valley between the Adirondacks of New York and the Green Mountains of Vermont, Suvir and his partner, Charlie, have found the perfect setting for living their passionate pursuits of cooking, designing kitchen equipment, farming, entertaining friends and family, and fulfilling their spiritual convictions of community and responsibility to the environment.

Suvir and Charlie contribute to the community in myriad ways. They provide products to new food ventures and offer advice and education, bringing in chefs from all over the country. In the nearby town of Salem, they also raise funds for the Battenkill Kitchen, to make available an affordable, qualified commercial kitchen for local cooks who want to sell their wares. They think nothing of jumping into the car to bring a crate of fresh farm eggs to Max London's restaurant in Saratoga Springs, an hour's drive away, because Max told them it wouldn't be Sunday brunch without those eggs. The croissants from Michael London's adjoining bakery—the best I've ever tasted—are photographed in the book as part of what has to be the ultimate bacon and egg sandwich.

We all want to succeed and be noticed, but for Suvir, becoming a better person comes first. Suvir's heritage of respect and reverence for people and all living things manifests itself at every turn. He comes from a culture where hospitality and concern for others are held sacred. It moved me to tears watching him politely saluting an elderly turbaned Hindu cab driver in New York, sweetly calling him Bhaisahib, seeing him graciously and attentively welcoming my ninety-six-year-old father to spend the night at his farm, and watching him relating to his farm's many animals.

American Masala Farm is welcoming to man, beast, and fowl alike. It provides a home to endangered species and those on the "critical list," such as Cayuga green-black ducks and American Buff geese, thirty-six breeds of chickens, two alpacas that were rejected by breeders (one for her endearingly comical buck teeth and the other for his neck that is a few inches too long), and the very rare Leicester Longwool sheep, originally brought to the United States by presidents Washington and Jefferson. One of Charlie and Suvir's goals for the future ". . . is our desire to start making cheese once we have at least a couple to three dozen girls in the flock."

There's an unequaled feeling of goodness—of connection to the earth—that comes from making jam and cooking regional produce that one forages, grows, or purchases from nearby farm stands. This is a land of wild raspberries on the roadside, wild mushrooms and animals in the nearby wooded hills, a state-protected trout stream, and a pond where the ducks and geese parade to and fro and their cousins the wild Canadian geese skid-land, feetfirst, during their annual migration.

In this extraordinary new book, Suvir merges his highly refined spice sensibility with the great produce of his adopted land. He also harvests favorite recipes from friends and worldwide travels such as the Farmhouse Crispy-Creamy Potatoes, roasted with herbs he cleverly calls Herbes de Hebron as a riff on herbes de Provence. And I was overjoyed to find the recipe for Roasted Manchurian Cauliflower, one of my favorite dishes at his New York City restaurant, Dévi—guaranteed to convert a professed detractor of the vegetable. Also gracing this book is a very special biscuit recipe—one that Suvir made for our breakfast and served with his homemade jams. The secret to these exceptionally tender and buttery biscuits is that compared to most, they have half the cream and double the butter! Consummate host that he is, Suvir sent my father home with an ample supply of biscuits and jam to enjoy in the comfort of his own home.

This book is blessed with many glorious photographs by the brilliantly talented Ben Fink; they illustrate the recipes and lifestyle that Suvir and Charlie share with sincere and engaging eloquence. For me, every word rings true because they perfectly reflect my two visits to the farm.

Once again, I saw the huge golden white rooster who prefers to hang out with the bucks (male goats) to his own hens but sits trustingly and contentedly in Suvir's embrace, and the alpacas whose lovely beige and brown furs become exquisitely soft yarn for knitting in the cold winter months and about whom Suvir says "They protect the goats and sheep, amuse us with their personalities, and enrich us with their fiber."

Suvir is one of those rare individuals who possesses a magnetic personality. All are drawn to him and want nothing more than to remain by his side to bask in the dynamic warmth, humor, generosity, and love that he radiates. But there is another side to Suvir—that of a sharply clever and playful master of the tease and please. He is full of surprises, and his recipes reflect all these enticing qualities. How wonderful to have this book by one's side from which to cook and to dream of an idyllic Masala Farm existence.

—Rose Levy Beranbaum, author of *The Cake Bible* and *Rose's Heavenly Cakes*

INTRODUCTION

City Boys, Country Masala

Live life with masala, and your mind, stomach, and spirit will always be satiated.

In Hindi, *masala* means "spice." In its simplest translation, *masala* is used to define a singular spice—like cinnamon or ground ginger—or a spice blend—like garam masala or *chaat* masala, a combination of spices that work together to create a symphony of taste explosions in even the simplest dish. Some flavors are bold and hit you immediately, while others only begin to entertain your taste buds seconds after you have taken the first bite. Then there are the lingering notes that hound you for hours after you have finished your meal, leaving you perplexed and pleased. Much like life, masala invites a combination of ups and downs, bitterness, spice, and sweetness that bring joy and interest to the every day.

With these contrasts, we can appreciate life with a greater sensibility. That's why masala is about much more than just adding flavor to food. It is about living—and appreciating—every moment of our lives. Exploring curiosities, being adventurous learners, sharing laughter and comforts with friends and family, traveling to expose yourself to new experiences, and eating food rich with character and spice—to me, *this* is living a life rich with masala.

And so with this book, I'm sharing masala-infused recipes and stories meant to entertain your minds, warm your hearts, and fill your bellies. It's my hope that you'll have a greater understanding of how to live a life charged with masala, and bring it into your kitchens and homes.

The glimmer of *Masala Farm* began after a weekend trip to a friend's farm in Vermont. My partner, Charlie Burd, and I started fantasizing about life in the country: a home with enough land to grow vegetables and fruit, to have a chicken coop and fresh farm eggs, to tend goats, and even to make cheese. We dreamt of how great it would be to create an environment where, like a great spice blend, people from all different backgrounds can mix together to share food, ideas, curiosities, and convictions.

After just a few short months of house hunting in 2005, Charlie and I found our home-to-be—a modest-size four-bedroom farmhouse with a gray slate roof and clapboard painted turmeric orange in upstate New York. With three ponds, a few barns, apple trees, and sixty-seven acres, it was perfect. (And I had no idea just how profound the effect would be on my cooking.) Our home, the American Masala Farm, has become a place where friends, chefs, and family from as near as next door or as far away as India can come to break bread, share stories, cook, and eat.

Our menus have become easier and more impromptu since moving here. This is a necessity, since we can never anticipate what is going to happen on the farm—a goat giving birth when we didn't even know she was pregnant, stolen goslings, coyotes in the goat pasture, a pump in the well on the fritz—anything can happen at any time. Cooking has also become a communal exercise. We are almost always entertaining, be it one guest or one dozen, and we enjoy getting everyone who will sit at the table involved in creating the meal. This gives everyone ownership, something to talk about and reflect upon, and stories for the next dinner. It also leads to a very informal and comforting energy in the kitchen. Anyone who may have been shy about his or her kitchen skills quickly abandons any sense of bashfulness and starts exchanging ideas, jokes, and gossip with the rest of us.

Having a farm has also connected me to the seasons, nature, and the elements in a way I hadn't experienced before. For instance, now I try to limit our foods to what's available from nearby farms as much as possible. This means cooking becomes local in spirit and communal in the labor involved, making the meal about today and the friends and neighbors who have gathered around the table. I open my menu to specialty ingredients, too. From Pat and Albert Sheldon of Sheldon Farms and from Meg and Rob Southerland of Gardenworks, we buy butter imported from Parma, Italy; Swiss Gruyère; and Spanish Marcona almonds, as well as seasonal berries and fresh vegetables. Their shops enrich our country lifestyles with amazing not-so-local products that crowd our pantry and make meals that much more special. We enjoy watching the shocked expression on friends' faces when they sit down to dinner at our table. Yes, we are farmers, and yes, we are in a rural setting, but we too have pantries with a global reach and gourmet ambitions. Dare I say we eat better north of Albany than we did in lower Manhattan? Rules and expectations have fallen by the wayside, and cooking has become as much about the joys of preparing a meal as it is about sitting down to relish it.

From the beginning, our plan was to use the property not as a weekend or summer retreat, like so many city-to-country transplants, but as our main residence. When many of our closest friends (and even some family members) heard this, they thought we had gone mad. How could two New York City boys who knew more about Prada than pitchforks possibly make it through a harsh country winter? Where would we do our grocery shopping in a place where sheep and goats certainly outnumber people? Would I finally learn how to drive a car, and if not, how would I expect to get around? In short, how would we survive?

Let's backtrack for a minute, to where my love of the country life began. I spent my childhood in New Delhi, India, in a modern home with every modern convenience. My brother, sister, and I went to private school and played cricket. My mother took care of us kids and, under careful instruction and tutelage from my paternal grandmother, she managed our home, which often entailed planning elaborate dinner parties for my father, a government bureaucrat, as well as for relatives. Panditji, my family's now retired yet still beloved and immensely gifted chef, was a fixture in our kitchen since long before I was born, and as far back as I can remember, I was his constant shadow. He taught me not just the ways of the kitchen but also, through his eyes, the ways of the world. During our time side by side at the stove, I learned about the world, religion, and the sanctity of life through his vivid stories and anecdotes. My favorites were about his country life in Faizabad, a village in the state of Uttar Pradesh. These tales sparked my fascination with rural India.

Then, when I was seven years old, my father was offered a teaching position in Nagpur in the northwestern state of Maharashtra. My family moved, yet Panditji, my teacher on so many levels, stayed behind to care for my grandmother's home in New Delhi, so Mom took over the cooking for company and for us kids. By India's standards, Nagpur, a city of a quarter million people, is thought of as being small and, in typical Indian fashion, had rural life endowed with chickens, goats, and cows, as well as rolling green hills and fields at every turn. I was enchanted by the nature of the city and routinely explored the hilly grounds around the stately manor we lived in, eager to have my own adventures to tell Panditji about.

After school one afternoon, I went exploring around the property and saw a beautiful baby goat alone in a field. It was love at first sight, and I decided to take her home with me. The frail little creature followed me to the house, and I created a bed for her from hay and fed her cereal, rice, and milk. That evening a man came to the house, asked for my father, and told him that one of his goats had gone missing. My father asked what he could do to help, and the farmer said, "Sir, I believe your son has taken my goat." Imagine my father's shock to walk into the garage and find me there with this humble farmer's goat! Of course, the farmer took back his goat—and ever since then, I have always wanted my own goat (though I never imagined being a parent to four dozen of them!).

Common sense is an important country trait, and the best role model in this realm was my practical mother. A wonderful cook, Mom took over the cooking detail while we lived in Nagpur. We visited Cotton Market every week to purchase exactly twenty-five eggs—enough for my siblings and me to each have our daily egg and with plenty left over for weekend cravings and treats, be they omelets or cakes. Mom's think-ahead approach to food and entertaining made it possible for us to eat regally for little cost and with little waste. She meticulously planned and rationed her ingredients, for it wasn't possible to run out to the corner market if her supplies were depleted. She kept a cooking journal that not only included the recipes and meals she made, but also to whom she served what dish and how much was left over at the end of the meal. In this way, whenever she had to entertain guests, she could easily open her journal, jot down the precise amount of ingredients she needed for the number of guests expected, and have neither too much nor too little to serve. In addition, she impressed many of her guests by never offering the same dish twice, or by serving select others their favorite dish on every visit.

In New Delhi, Panditji taught me about traditions, classic dishes, and the history behind them; in Nagpur, Mom gave me an education in how to be a practical, savvy, and creative cook and host. And it was in Nagpur that I developed my fascination for farm animals like chickens and goats. I like to think that my cooking style today is a mishmash of these big influences.

Goats were a part of our everyday life in India, and while my childhood desire to raise a goat went unfulfilled, Charlie and I are more than making up for it now. We tend to our small herd with as much care and tenderness as I did as a boy, petting them, feeding them, and attending to them as the special, gentle, and smart creatures they are. Now that I have my own herd of LaManchas (plus an Angora goat and a few Oberhasli crossbreeds that are pets and don't produce milk), I find that using the goats' milk in my cooking is a grounding experience that connects me to the food chain and to India, reminding me that milk doesn't come from cardboard cartons but from healthy, loved animals. This affection for farm animals has given me more strength to come to terms with the fact that many of the animals we are nurturing and caring for will end up on a dinner table at either our home or at my restaurant, Dévi, in New York City.

Now that I live in the country, I am forced to be smart about meal planning like Mom was, and like Panditji, I strive to wow and excite my guests, stimulate their senses, and stoke their appetites with the smell of toasted cumin, the color of bright saffron, and the spice of the Indian kitchen. I am constantly applying these lessons learned from my elders to my cooking at the farm.

In the summer when fresh berries and just-picked veggies are plentiful, it is heaven to have a country kitchen. I make thick blueberry jam from the berries that grow right outside my back door (as well as from the ones purchased at nearby farms) and an herby tomato marinara with the heirloom fruits from my garden. Finding inspiration isn't difficult—it's there in my garden, in our neighbors' gardens, at the farmers' markets, and dangling from the trees.

Besides writing cookbooks and running the restaurant, I am the chairperson of the Culinary Institute of America's Asian Studies program, and as such I am constantly on the go, traveling across America promoting the flavors of India. I find travel and teaching completely inspiring and educational, and through my students' questions and cooking anecdotes, I learn how they incorporate masala into their lives.

But although I thrive on educating those new to Indian spices, as well as Indophiles, about how to heighten the flavor of their favorite dishes with a few herbs, spices, or techniques, there is nothing more satisfying than returning home, where I turn off my BlackBerry, give e-mail a rest, and enjoy living and cooking in the country. When I come home from these teaching trips, my muscles untangle, my mind clears. As soon as the car brakes onto the gravel drive, I'm off, camera in hand, rushing to check on my girls—our 120-plus heritage-breed chickens.

We have a stunning assortment of chickens, like brown-spotted Buttercups with fiery orange-plumed necks and Silver-Spangled Hamburgs that look like the chicken incarnate of a Dalmatian. I love these coiffed divas and have taken to religiously documenting their lives on the farm through snapshots: walking through the fields, perching on a stump, peeking out the coop window. Once they realize that I'm an innocuous presence, some will even rest on my shoulder. The visit culminates in checking for eggs, collecting them in a bowl, and using them for that night's egg curry dinner or in a simple breakfast scramble the next morning.

After visiting the chickens, I'll check on one of my favorite goats, Geoffrey, who was a gift from Angela Miller, my literary agent and the proprietor of Consider Bardwell Farm in Vermont just fifteen minutes over the state line from us. Geoffrey has an incredible disposition and is friendly beyond what you would ever imagine possible for a goat. Charlie and I were so taken with his personality that we altered our original plan for the farm, deciding to raise goats instead of sheep, assuming that all goats would have what we like to call the Geoffrey gene (which we ultimately discovered they don't). Needless to say, we still enjoy the fresh goat's milk that we drink in our coffee and chai, turn into caramely *cajeta*, and cook with, too.

Sometimes after a trip away, I find myself hungry for the stunning just-harvested produce available at our many neighboring farm stands. Charlie and I might drive down Route 22 and supplement the bounty from our garden with that from Sheldon Farms, where we always buy sublime butter and sugar-sweet corn, as well as purple-speckled cranberries, green heirloom beans, and just-dug potatoes. We'll often stop off at Gardenworks to add to our own harvest of blueberries and, if it's a Sunday, maybe the farmers' market in Dorset to visit some of our favorite produce farmers, cheesemakers, and meat purveyors. On the way home, we'll swing by Battenkill Valley Creamery, where we'll leave a few dollars in the cash box (they still work by the honor system) and pull some heavy cream (thicker and creamier than you could imagine), whole milk, or their incredible chocolate milk from the reach-in cooler.

During the wintertime, it's a different story. Aside from my beloved chickens that produce eggs for our enjoyment year-round, there is no local harvest to support and visit. I am confined to the bounty of my cold storage and that of the local supermarket, which, I must say, has gotten much better throughout the years, now offering imported cheeses and other "gourmet" food items. Though it is massive in size, this supermarket is a far cry from the quality and selection of winter produce to which I was accustomed in Manhattan. These cold months are when my creativity really goes into overdrive and, like Mom in Nagpur, I have found that with little means I can make delicious meals.

My cooking has become more practical and less off-the-cuff than it once was. In New York City, dinner and groceries were always just a few steps from my front door. But in the country, food shopping happens far less often and must sustain meals over several days. This is to conserve fuel, our energy (rising at sunup with the chickens takes it toll), and my relationship with Charlie (since I don't have a driver's license, he's the one who gets to shuttle me thirty miles to and from the store). During winter, I've learned to rely on the local supermarket for fruits and vegetables and on my stocked pantry for spices, dried beans, rice, and legumes, as well as the canned chutneys, jams, and vegetables that I preserved during the summer's months of plenty.

Divided by seasons, the recipes in *Masala Farm* reflect our rural life. What each recipe has in common is my unique approach to introducing spice and excitement to food in unexpected ways. For example, deviled eggs (see recipe, page 74) get a dose of Indian *sambhaar* powder (similar to what many call "curry powder") as well as a jalapeño for spice and crème fraîche for richness, while a fresh country ham (see recipe, page 58) gets a rubdown with soy sauce and rice wine before it heads into the oven for the better part of an afternoon. Enhancing flavors of classic recipes by introducing unexpected finishing oils, spice blends, marinades, rubs, and seasonings are the trademarks of my cooking. By offering the simplest twist on a classic recipe, like adding freshly ground black pepper to a quiche crust or fresh ginger and saffron to rhubarb jam, I'm serving up a new version of a traditional recipe that is at once deliciously modern yet still comforting and recognizable.

In each chapter, you'll find a multitude of approachable, doable recipes, always light on the fuss and big on the flavor, using Indian techniques and flavors that bring an exciting freshness to the table. You'll also gain insight into the comedy and honest reality of our everyday lives, as well as the Washington County community that we have become a part of and love dearly. This is the American countryside, masala style.

CHAPTER ONE

SPRING

Anticipation, Patience,
and Delicious Rewards

The animals are the first to alert us that spring is here. After taking shelter in the barns throughout many months of cold and snow, they get spring fever big time and ache to explore the land. The goats, sheep, and alpacas head to the pasture, and the ducks and geese make a beeline to the barns, where they gather hay to make nests for their soon-to-come babies.

When the geese and ducks first begin laying their eggs, Charlie and I take their eggs for selfish reasons—like frittatas, quiche, and banana pudding, to name a few. The geese will hiss when we come close to their nests, and then they do the funniest thing—they either roll over or get up and walk away! We grab the eggs and, easy as that, our morning "shopping" is done. Friends make special trips from afar just to get a taste of our fresh chicken, duck, and goose eggs from shells in the most beautiful colors, teal and pale gray-blue pastels to earthy clay hues and rose-tinted browns. Year-round we sell some of our bounty to Mrs. London's and Max London's, a bakery and restaurant respectively, in Saratoga Springs. They turn our eggs into a topping for an amazing mushroom and taleggio pizza or serve them alongside duck confit hash. In the springtime, just before Easter, they adorn the eggs with gold leaf and gold powder highlights. Instantly, our simple farm eggs become as chic as can be.

This is the season of bread and eggs for breakfast, lunch, and dinner. Giant goose eggs (one goose egg is equal in size to about four chicken eggs) and duck eggs, plus eggs from our heritage-breed chickens, are all in abundance beginning in the spring. With a shell that can seem as tough as porcelain, a goose egg requires a lot of effort to crack, but the result is worth the work. My favorite way to serve these mammoth beauties is fried with fruity olive oil and ground peppercorns and then finished with freshly grated Parmigiano-Reggiano cheese. They are incredible served alongside butter-basted skillet biscuits (I bake them nearly every morning at the farm). By the end of March we stop stealing the duck and goose eggs, and let the girls keep them so that they can hatch into the adorable fuzz-covered babies that will soon waddle around the lawns. From this point on, we collect eggs from the henhouse to sate our addiction.

Another spring highlight is maple syrup. During our first winter thaw in the North Country, I noticed hundreds of blue pipes mushrooming from trees throughout the countryside. I had no idea that these pipes were used to tap trees for maple syrup, one of the biggest sources of revenue for our community. We don't have any syrup-producing maples on our property, but many of our friends do, and they gift us fresh maple syrup (we reciprocate with homemade Spiced Rhubarb Jam, page 63, or other Seasonal Jam, page 109, later in the year).

One of our greatest joys is hosting events to benefit various local charities. One such organization we support is the Agricultural Stewardship Association (ASA), a non-profit dedicated to protecting farmland in the upper Hudson Valley and preserving it for future generations. Just as the lilacs fill the air with their genteel perfume and the spring bulbs have bloomed with a vengeance, we gather at the farm for an annual ASA benefit. The community comes together to enjoy the new gifts of the season, like hardy greens and new garlic, and to relish the last of the hard squash, carrots, potatoes, apples, and pears from the cold cellar. I serve a mix of Indian and American country foods, as well as dishes inspired by my travels, like Ginger-Soy Fresh Ham with Roasted Garlic (page 58), meatloaf, goat kebabs, Farmhouse Crispy-Creamy Potatoes (page 43), and Banana-Caramel Pudding (page 60). It's a celebration of rebirth and renewal, of old ways, and of delicious food, of course.

GOAT CHEESE AND HERB FRITTATA

Serves 4

4 oz/115 g fresh creamy chèvre (or brebis blanche or fromage blanc)

¼ cup/60 ml heavy cream

4 duck eggs (or 6 large chicken eggs)

4 tbsp/10 g finely chopped fresh herbs (like basil, lemon verbena, parsley, rosemary, winter savory, tarragon, and thyme)

1 tsp kosher salt

2 tbsp extra-virgin olive oil

1 tsp freshly ground black pepper

2 shallots, finely chopped

You can't imagine how exciting it is when we make our first spring frittata with fresh-laid eggs from our ducks. We use just-made crottin de chèvre from Consider Bardwell Farm, a few miles from the house, and young, tender sprigs of herbs we pluck from the seedlings that we've grown indoors (they won't be ready to transplant until the danger of frost subsides in May). This frittata is a celebration of spring's firsts that wakes up our palate from a long winter of cabbage, squash, and stew.

❁ ❁ ❁

Adjust one oven rack to the upper-middle position and leave one oven rack in the center position. Heat the oven to 350°F/180°C/gas 4. Place three-quarters of the chèvre in a medium bowl and whisk or mash it using a rubber spatula to loosen it up. Add the cream and whisk until it is relatively smooth. Add the eggs, 3 tbsp of the herbs, and the salt. Whisk until the mixture is smooth and well combined.

Heat the olive oil with the pepper in an 8-in/20-cm oven-safe heavy-bottomed frying pan over medium-high heat until the pepper is fragrant, about 30 seconds. Stir in the remaining herbs and fry until they become fragrant, about 30 seconds, and then add the shallots and cook, stirring often, until they are soft and translucent, 2 to 3 minutes.

Pour the egg mixture over the shallots. Reduce the heat to low, give the mixture a stir, and then let it cook just until it begins to set up on top (the underside will be cooked and the upper portion won't be runny but will still have some gloss), 8 to 10 minutes.

Transfer the frying pan to the oven and cook until it just begins to puff, about 5 minutes. Pull out, and sprinkle with the remaining chèvre. Place the frittata back into the oven to cook until the chèvre is warmed through, about 3 minutes longer. Turn on the broiler and broil the frittata until there are dark spots on the cheese, 30 seconds to 1½ minutes. Slice into wedges and serve.

CAULIFLOWER, CHÈVRE, AND ONION QUICHE

We are blessed with an abundance of eggs in the springtime—chicken eggs, duck eggs, goose eggs, you name it. People come to our house during this time of year craving our golden, fluffy Goat Cheese and Herb Frittata (facing page), but there are only so many frittatas I can make before I'm frittata-ed out! That is when I turn to quiche. Enriched with Gruyère and fresh chèvre and encased in a rosemary-flavored buttery crust, quiche is an excellent make-ahead dish that can feed many. Like a frittata, the variations are limited only by your imagination—I've added everything from leftover roasted vegetables to Indian-spiced green peas embossed with garam masala. Dress it up with a simple salad of leafy greens, or make it heartier by serving it with our Farmhouse Crispy-Creamy Potatoes (page 43) on the side.

Serves 6 to 8

FOR THE PASTRY

6 tbsp/85 g unsalted butter, plus 1 tbsp at room temperature

1⅔ cups/200 g all-purpose flour, plus extra for rolling

2 tsp finely chopped fresh rosemary

¾ tsp kosher salt or fleur de sel

1 egg yolk

FOR THE FILLING

3 tbsp extra-virgin olive oil

1 tsp freshly ground black pepper

2 tbsp finely chopped fresh herbs (any combination of chives, rosemary, tarragon, thyme, or winter savory)

½ large red onion, halved and thinly sliced

1½ tsp kosher salt

1 small or ½ large head cauliflower, divided into small florets

5 large eggs

8 oz/225 g Gruyère cheese, grated (about 2 cups)

3 oz/85 g fresh chèvre

2 tbsp finely chopped fresh flat-leaf parsley

❋ ❋ ❋

To make the pastry: Slice the 6 tbsp/85 g butter into small pieces, place them in a bowl, and put in the freezer to chill. In a food processor, pulse together the flour, rosemary, and salt. In a small bowl, whisk the egg yolk with 3 tbsp cold water and set aside. Add the cold butter to the flour mixture and pulse until the dry ingredients are mealy with nuggets no larger than a small pea. Pulse in the liquid just until the dry ingredients look sandy, then turn the mixture out onto your worksurface. Knead the mixture lightly until it can be pressed into a mound (if you tap it, it should break apart). Transfer the mound to a large sheet of plastic wrap, wrap it tightly, and then lightly knead the dough to make a solid, flat disc. Chill the dough for at least 45 minutes or up to 3 days.

Preheat the oven to 400°F/200°C/gas 6. Unwrap the dough and place it on a generously floured worksurface. Roll the dough to a 10-in/25-cm circle, fold it into quarters, and transfer it to a 9-in/23-cm extra-deep pie dish, a 9½-in/24-cm standard pie dish, or a 10-in/25-cm fluted tart pan with removable bottom. Fit the dough into the corners of the pan and, if using a pie dish, trim and crimp the edges (if using a tart pan with removable bottom, press off the excess dough to create a clean edge). Chill the dough for 30 minutes.

continued ...

Rub the remaining 1 tbsp butter over a large sheet of aluminum foil. Line the chilled pie crust with the foil, buttered-side down, and then line the foil with pie weights or dried beans. Bake the pie crust until it is just set, about 12 minutes. Remove it from the oven and remove the foil and weights. Place the crust back in the oven and continue to bake until it is golden, about 5 minutes longer. Remove from the oven and set aside.

To make the filling: In a large frying pan, heat the olive oil, black pepper, and herbs over medium-high heat until the herbs are fragrant, about 30 seconds. Stir in the onion and ½ tsp of the salt and cook, stirring often, until the onion is browned and starting to crisp, about 8 minutes. Add the cauliflower and cook until browned and glossy and the onion starts to stick to the bottom of the pan, 4 to 5 minutes. Turn off the heat and set aside to cool slightly.

In a large bowl, whisk the eggs with the Gruyère, chèvre, parsley, and remaining salt. Scrape the vegetables into the crust, and then pour the egg-cheese mixture over the vegetables. Place the quiche on a rimmed baking sheet and bake until the filling is browned, slightly puffy, and set, 30 to 40 minutes. Let cool for at least 30 minutes before removing the rings, slicing, and serving.

FARM❋YARN

GOAT'S MILK SURPRISE

It's been our experience that most people are squeamish about trying goat's milk. Whenever we ask our guests if they'd like to drink some, they often respond as if we'd just offered them brains for breakfast: gaping mouths, wide eyes, and raised eyebrows. So we no longer ask . . . we surprise.

Spring is the time of year when the goats have their babies and the mothers produce milk to feed them. After the kids are weaned, Charlie gets up early to milk the goats and brings the fresh unpasteurized, non-homogenized milk in to the fridge. Around the time that Charlie returns to the house with the milk is about the same time our guests—we're always playing host to someone—usually start descending from the second floor, awake and ready for coffee and a hearty breakfast.

Right away we ask our guests if they would like to try some goat's milk, as fresh as the day is young. They inevitably respond with shocked looks, and we don't press them any further. Instead, Charlie innocently places a pitcher of milk on the counter. Our friends make themselves coffee with, yes, the goat's milk. They admire the milk for its richness, its creaminess, it's fresh flavor. . . . Charlie and I smirk and look at them with knowing eyes . . . and then they guess the truth—it's goat's milk!

In a blind taste test, most people actually prefer the goat's milk to the cow's. Besides its wonderful flavor, it's more digestible and has less fat. Our country neighbors need no convincing. These characters swing by the farm in the morning knowing that we will have an extra jug or two of milk to give to them.

SCRATCH BEAN SALAD WITH BASIL AND ROASTED PEPPERS

Serves 8

1 lb/455 g dried beans

2½ tsp kosher salt

1 tbsp unsalted butter

½ tsp Herbes de Hebron (page 215) or herbes de Provence

½ tsp freshly ground black pepper, plus extra for serving

⅛ tsp red pepper flakes

2 medium carrots, peeled and finely diced

2½ tbsp extra-virgin olive oil, plus extra for serving

1½ tbsp red wine vinegar

½ medium red onion, finely chopped

3 roasted red bell peppers, seeded and diced into ¼-in/6-mm pieces

2 tbsp grated Parmigiano-Reggiano cheese, plus extra for serving

¼ cup/10 g thinly sliced fresh basil leaves

Chef Cesare Casella, the chef-owner of the fantastic Salumeria Rosi on the Upper West Side of Manhattan, and his wife, Eileen, gave us a wonderful selection of heirloom Italian beans from their company, Republic of Beans. What did we do with the beautiful selection of Italian heritage beans fagioli pavoni, scritti, fagioli del papa, coco di mamma, pavoni, cicerchi, fagioli corona, *and* fagioli diavoli? *We put them in decorative jars to give shape and color to our curio display. Shameless!*

After more time than I care to admit, Charlie and I realized that we had to cook them, otherwise we'd bear the wrath of Cesare (whose wrath is about as fearsome as a teddy bear's). We came up with this salad inspired by a version that Cesare served us when we first met him while he was the chef at Beppe (and later Maremma) in New York City. It's about the texture of the beans, the fruitiness of the olive oil, and the pungency of the basil. Try to get the best-quality dried beans you can (see Farmhouse Resources, page 222), meaning plump and shiny, not shriveled and dull. Herbs and black pepper gently fried in olive oil (a classic Indian technique) boost the flavor of this otherwise simply seasoned salad.

❀ ❀ ❀

Place the beans in a stockpot and cover with 6 in/15.25 cm warm water. Bring to a boil, reduce the heat to low, and cook until the beans are plump but not entirely cooked through, about 1 hour (cook the beans on low heat so that they retain their shape). Add 1 tsp of the salt and continue cooking until the beans are tender, 1 to 2 hours longer (depending on the size of the beans and how fresh they are). Drain the beans in a colander and transfer them to a large bowl.

Melt the butter in a large frying pan over medium heat. Add the Herbes de Hebron, black pepper, and red pepper flakes and cook until fragrant, stirring often, about 1 minute. Stir in the carrots and ½ tsp salt and cook until the carrots are tender, stirring often, 5 to 7 minutes. Turn off the heat and transfer the seasoned carrots to the bowl with the beans.

Whisk together the olive oil and vinegar and immediately drizzle it over the beans and carrots, then stir to combine. Stir in the onion, roasted peppers, Parmigiano-Reggiano, basil, and remaining 1 tsp salt. Taste and season with salt if needed, and add a drizzle more oil if the beans taste dry. Serve warm, at room temperature, or cold with extra Parmigiano-Reggiano, a drizzle of olive oil, and freshly ground black pepper.

VARIATION: BEAN SOUP

Transfer half of the bean salad to a food processor and blend with 3 to 4 cups/720 to 950 ml of water, chicken broth, or vegetable broth until smooth. Scrape the mixture into a large pot and repeat with the remaining beans. If you like a chunkier bean soup, leave the second batch of beans at more of a rough texture than the first. Scrape the second half of the processed beans into the pot. Cook over medium heat until hot, adjust with more water or broth, and season with salt and pepper. Serve finished with a sprinkle of freshly grated Parmigiano-Reggiano, a drizzle of fruity olive oil, and a crack of pepper.

RECIPE NOTE: PLANNED OVERS

Charlie and I like to say that we don't have leftovers in our house, we have "planned overs." Meaning, I double or even triple a recipe, such as with this bean salad. I'll take some of the planned overs and toss them with warm pasta for a rustic lunch, and then purée the rest with water to make a voluminous and richly flavored bean soup (see Variation above). Or I'll prepare the salad as a white bean hummus spread by puréeing it in the food processor along with a little water, olive oil, and fresh lemon juice and serve it like bruschetta on a slice of toasted baguette. There is no harm in repurposing leftovers. Getting many meals from one pot of beans is pure country ingenuity!

PASTA
PRIMAVERA

Serves 6

1 tbsp kosher salt, plus 1½ tsp

One 14.5-oz/410-g box of whole-grain, multigrain, or nutrient-enriched penne pasta (or other tube or spiral-shaped pasta)

9 tbsp/135 ml extra-virgin olive oil

3 dried red chiles

1 sprig fresh rosemary

1 tsp freshly ground black pepper

1 medium red onion, halved and thinly sliced

1 medium head (about 2 lb/910 g) cauliflower, divided into small florets

10 oz/280 g brown mushrooms, stemmed and thinly sliced

3 garlic cloves, coarsely chopped

¼ cup/10 g finely chopped fresh basil leaves

2 tbsp unsalted butter

1 cup/100 g finely grated Parmigiano-Reggiano cheese

Charlie's Grandmother Burd from West Virginia travels to our farm a few times a year. During these visits, we know we have to be at the top of our game, because this woman is tireless—she's five feet tall, in her mid-eighties, and makes us look like lumps of lazy corruption! She loves to pick our herbs and vegetables (and then watches me like a hawk to make sure I use each and every one she has gathered). This pasta primavera is the result of one such garden adventure. You can use any vegetables you like in this recipe, just remember to add the quicker-cooking tender vegetables toward the end so that they don't overcook.

❀ ❀ ❀

Bring a large pot of water to a boil. Add the 1 tbsp salt and the pasta, and cook until the pasta is al dente. Drain and set aside.

Heat 4 tbsp/60 ml of the olive oil with the chiles, rosemary, and black pepper in a large heavy-bottomed pan over medium heat until the rosemary becomes fragrant, about 30 seconds. Add the onion and 1½ tsp salt and cook, stirring often, until the onion is limp and brown around the edges, 5 to 8 minutes.

Push the onion to the side of the pan and add another 2 tbsp olive oil and the cauliflower. Stir the cauliflower into the oil (but not into the onion pushed over to the side) and cook, stirring often, until the florets start to brown and become soft, about 5 minutes. (If the cauliflower browns too quickly, reduce the heat to medium-low.)

Push the cauliflower to the side and add another 2 tbsp olive oil and the mushrooms. Mix together all the vegetables, and cook until the mushrooms become glossy and shriveled, about 2 minutes.

Make a hole in the center of the vegetables and add the remaining 1 tbsp olive oil and the garlic. Cook until the garlic becomes fragrant, 30 seconds to 1 minute, and then stir the garlic into the rest of the vegetables. Cook all the vegetables together for 3 minutes and then stir in the basil and the cooked pasta. Reduce the heat to low, add the butter and, once it is melted, stir in the Parmigiano-Reggiano. Taste, add more salt if necessary, and serve.

ASPARAGUS AND GREEN PEA
RISOTTO WITH FRESH HERB TARKA

*In India, we look to add flavor to food using spices and cooking techniques,
not stock. So instead of weighing down risotto with chicken broth, I instead
fry herbs in butter and oil to make a tarka, a seasoned oil stirred into food
to brighten its flavor. But I like a good stock, too, and I make mine with
every scrap of vegetable when I cook, meaning that the carrot peelings,
mushroom stems, and asparagus ends become stock for the risotto, introducing depth, nutrition, and interest beyond what plain water can bring.
Making water-based scrap stocks also helps control the sodium levels
of the finished dish (read the nutrition label on that can of chicken broth
and be prepared for a shock when you get to the percent of sodium that one
serving of the packaged broth adds to your daily intake). A Parmigiano-
Reggiano rind or a few whole black peppercorns add a nice extra flavor.*

❁ ❁ ❁

To make the tarka: Melt the butter in a medium frying pan over medium
heat. Add the olive oil, basil, rosemary, thyme, black pepper, and red
pepper flakes. Cook, stirring often, until the mixture is fragrant, about
1 minute. Turn off the heat and set aside.

To make the risotto: Snap off the tough ends of the asparagus and add
them to a large soup pot. Slice the trimmed asparagus spears on the
diagonal into 1-in/2.5-cm lengths, leave the tips whole, and place both
in a medium bowl and set aside.

Pour 12 cups/2.85 L water over the asparagus ends and add 1 tsp of the
salt, the Parmigiano-Reggiano rind (if using), and the coarsely ground
pepper (if using). Bring the liquid to a boil over medium-high heat,
reduce the heat to medium-low, cover, and gently simmer until the broth
is fragrant, about 25 minutes. Strain the broth into a clean pot, cover
to keep the broth warm, and discard the asparagus ends and the rind.
(The broth can be made up to a week in advance; reheat before making
the risotto.) You should have about 10 cups/2.35 L broth.

continued . . .

Serves 8

FOR THE TARKA

2 tbsp unsalted butter

2 tbsp extra-virgin olive oil

1 tbsp finely chopped fresh basil

1 tsp finely chopped fresh rosemary

1 tsp finely chopped fresh thyme

¼ tsp freshly ground black pepper

⅛ tsp red pepper flakes

FOR THE RISOTTO

2 lb/910 g asparagus

2 tsp kosher salt

1 Parmigiano-Reggiano rind
(optional), plus 1 cup/100 g finely
grated Parmigiano-Reggiano cheese

1 tsp coarsely ground pepper
(optional), plus 1 tsp freshly ground
black pepper

6 tbsp/85 g unsalted butter

1 medium red onion, finely chopped

2 cups/200 g Arborio rice

½ cup/120 ml dry white wine

10-oz/280-g bag fresh or frozen
green peas

Finely chopped fresh basil
for serving

Melt the butter in a large heavy-bottomed pot over medium-high heat. Add the freshly ground pepper and cook, stirring often, until fragrant, about 30 seconds. Stir in the onion and ½ tsp salt and cook, stirring often, until the onion is translucent and soft, 1½ to 2 minutes. Add the rice and cook, stirring often, until the grains are opaque, 1½ to 2 minutes. Pour in the wine and cook, stirring often, until it is absorbed, 1 to 2 minutes. Reduce the heat to medium and add 1 cup/240 ml of the broth. Cook the risotto, stirring constantly, until the liquid is mostly absorbed (when you push a wooden spoon through the center of the pot, a trail should remain for 1 second before the rice comes back together) and then add another 1 cup/240 ml of warm broth. The rice will probably need about 2 minutes of cooking and stirring between each addition.

Once you have added 5 cups/1.18 L broth total to the risotto (after about 10 minutes), add the sliced asparagus, asparagus tips, peas, and the remaining ½ tsp salt. You know the risotto is done when the rice is creamy, not mushy, the grains are plump yet separate, and the rice is cooked to an al dente doneness (there should be an opaque speck in the center of a grain of rice), after another three to five additions of broth and 8 to 10 minutes more. Turn off the heat. Add the tarka and 2 tbsp of the Parmigiano-Reggiano, stirring to combine. Spoon the risotto into serving bowls, shower with some fresh basil and Parmigiano-Reggiano, and serve.

FARMHOUSE CRISPY-CREAMY POTATOES

Anne Willan's book From My Château Kitchen *and her recipe for butter-and-oil-poached and roasted potatoes are partially responsible for getting us out of the city and into the country. We fell in love with her stories about her elegant country life and made her creamy olive oil–poached potatoes over and over again in our tiny Manhattan kitchen, and then in our generous farmhouse one. Throughout the years, we've played with her recipe, combining it with Charlie's Grandmother Hayes's method, which involves parboiling the potatoes first and finishing them in a cast-iron frying pan. The resulting potatoes are wonderfully crisp on the outside with soufflé-like interiors. I add whole heads of garlic and loads of herbs that infuse the potatoes and the oil. Like most Indians, I have a deep love of carbohydrates, and I'm famous for serving the potatoes alongside fresh-baked bread for smearing the roasted garlic on—pure indulgence! Herbes de Hebron is my take on herbes de Provence—blending your own spices is economical and practical, yielding a brighter flavor than preblended mixes. If you prefer, you can use preblended herbes de Provence.*

Serves 6

1 tbsp kosher salt

1 lb/455 g medium red potatoes, halved

1 tsp Herbes de Hebron (page 215) or herbes de Provence

5 tbsp/70 g unsalted butter

1 cup/240 ml canola oil

⅓ cup/80 ml extra-virgin olive oil

11 fresh sage leaves

1½ sprigs fresh rosemary

1½ sprigs fresh thyme

2 heads garlic, top one-third cut off so cloves are exposed

❀ ❀ ❀

Bring a large pot of cold water and 2 tsp of the salt to a boil. Add the potatoes and Herbes de Hebron and return to a boil. Reduce the heat to medium and simmer until a paring knife easily slips into the center, about 15 minutes. Drain through a sieve and set the potatoes aside.

Preheat the oven to 350°F/180°C/gas 4. Melt the butter in a large cast-iron frying pan over medium heat. Add the canola oil and olive oil, 8 sage leaves, 1 sprig rosemary, and 1 sprig thyme. Carefully turn the potatoes into the frying pan and bring the liquid to a simmer. Turn off the heat and place the pan in the oven for 30 minutes. Remove the frying pan from the oven and add the garlic along with the remaining 3 sage leaves, ½ sprig rosemary, and ½ sprig thyme. Sprinkle with the remaining 1 tsp salt. Return the pan to the oven and continue to roast until the potatoes are deeply browned and crisp and the garlic is tender, another 30 to 45 minutes. Remove from the oven and let cool for 10 minutes before serving. Be sure to offer a few roasted garlic cloves along with each serving of potatoes.

WARM EGG SALAD ON CROISSANTS WITH COUNTRY BACON AND ARUGULA

This is basic country food at its finest. Lisa Smith, the executive chef for Central Market supermarkets in Texas, was visiting us at the farm, and one morning we brought her to Max London's in Saratoga Springs for breakfast. Their croissants blew her away and she called them the best she ever had (and Lisa knows croissants—she studied under the wonderfully gifted chef-teacher Madeleine Kamman and worked in France). She bought a few to bring back to the house and, upon arrival, said to Charlie and me, "Guys, today you rest. I'm making egg salad for lunch!" Of course, Lisa's egg salad isn't just egg salad—it's creamy and warm and punctuated by the slight bite and crunch of arugula and smoky country bacon.

❋ ❋ ❋

Preheat the oven to 350°F/180°C/gas 4. Lay the bacon on a rimmed baking sheet and cook in the oven for 10 to 20 minutes, depending on how crisp you like your bacon. Remove the pan from the oven and use tongs to transfer the bacon to a paper towel–lined plate to drain and cool. Set aside. Reduce the oven temperature to 200°F/95°C.

Pour the water and vinegar into a large pot and bring to a boil over high heat. Reduce the heat to medium and use a slotted spoon to gently lower the eggs into the boiling water. Simmer the eggs (reduce the heat to medium-low if necessary) for exactly 12 minutes.

While the eggs cook, set the croissants on a rimmed baking sheet and place them in the oven to warm (reassemble the croissants so they are whole—you don't want the interiors to get toasty and hard).

Transfer the cooked eggs to a sieve and place them under cold running water until they're cool enough to handle (you don't want the eggs to be cold—they need to be warm). Peel the eggs, place them in the bowl of a food processor, and purée until they're creamy. Add the mayonnaise, season with salt and pepper, and continue to process until the mixture is well combined.

Divide the egg salad among the bottom halves of the croissants. Top each with 4 pieces of arugula and 2 pieces of bacon. Cover with the top halves of the croissants and eat immediately.

Serves 4

8 strips good-quality thick-cut bacon

8 cups/2 L water

¼ cup/60 ml white vinegar

8 large eggs, at room temperature

4 butter croissants, halved

¼ cup/60 ml mayonnaise, store-bought or homemade (page 217)

Kosher salt

Freshly ground black pepper

16 leaves baby arugula

FARM ✽ YARN

DROP-INS WELCOME!

Part of the fun of having an open-door farmhouse is that we never know who is going to stop by. One afternoon, it could be an Emmy Award-winning television director; another day, it could be a narcotic-toting hippie. While all is quiet during the winter, spring is the time when people start stopping by—announced, unannounced, and sometimes even unbeknownst to us. Often it's the baby goats and the goslings that draw them in. Other times it's just our wooden sign for fresh farm eggs.

One morning, a seemingly nice-enough guy stopped by the farm asking about our eggs. Charlie explained that heritage birds are heirloom chickens, that they're not commercially bred to lay eggs religiously, that they lay eggs in a rainbow of colors, et cetera. He also told the stranger how much we charge for a dozen ($5 in the country, $10 in the city). Then the man asked Charlie for a few samples. This odd request took Charlie by surprise. It's not cheap to raise and house the chickens, and we generally keep the eggs for ourselves or sell them to very appreciative friends and locals. A sample? Nearly unheard of! But Charlie, being the generous soul he

is, went to the henhouse, pulled a few eggs, and handed them over. The man responded, "Thanks for the eggs. Here, let me give you a joint!"

On another occasion, during our first spring at the farmhouse, I noticed a man trespassing on our land near the stream. Any other morning, I might have blown off the incident—especially since our stream is a sight to behold this time of year with Canada geese, wood ducks, blue herons, and other wild animals enjoying the water—but it just so happened that we had just purchased our "protection" (yes, a gun—see "Lock, Stock, and Two Smoking Barrels," page 146, for the story behind that one), and I was a tad on edge because of it. So Charlie and I put on our most menacing scowls and stomped to the stream in our bathrobes and slippers. We approached the man and asked him what he was doing. He said that for the past few years, he had come to our stream every spring to fish for trout. We told him that this is fine with us, just to please let us know in the future. Charlie and I crunched through the dry grass back to the house and went about our business. At the end of the day, we had a lovely gift awaiting us on the porch—six glistening, freshly caught, scaled, and gutted freshwater trout from our own stream. This man and his gift of trout have now become, like the returning geese, a sign of spring's welcome return.

Uninvited visitors also come in the form of animals. In this case, ravens. It all started when Charlie and I were in London, where we fell in love with the beautiful inky birds that called the Tower of London home. Back on the farm, we prayed for ravens and, miraculously, they arrived! We were so excited to watch the beautiful, glorious creatures coast through the sky. And then one day I saw a flying raven carrying one of our precious goslings in its beak and I looked on in horror as it dropped the baby to its death. My heart sank and my eyes welled with tears. We lost about forty-five baby ducks and geese to those black birds that year.

Now, we try to one-up nature. We steal the babies from the mothers the very minute they emerge from the shells and bring them into the coop so they might have a better chance at survival. We don't want to shoot the ravens—they weren't spotted for a long time in our area—so it is a somewhat melancholy excitement with which we now greet them. It's gratifying to see an endangered bird, but not so gratifying when that endangered bird goes and kills one of my endangered birds! Such is the reality, the double-edged sword of spring, and the vagaries of farm life.

MARYANN'S STUFFED GRAPE LEAVES

Makes 50 to 60 dolmas

½ cup/95 g long-grain rice

50 to 60 fresh or jarred grape leaves (preferably Orlando brand)

5 large yellow onions, very finely chopped

½ cup/70 g toasted pine nuts

½ cup/85 g raisins

½ cup/120 ml fresh lemon juice (from 2 to 4 lemons)

¼ cup/60 ml canola or grapeseed oil

¼ cup/60 ml extra-virgin olive oil

I tbsp sugar

I tbsp plus I tsp kosher salt

¼ tsp freshly ground black pepper

Pomegranate seeds for serving

Fresh dill fronds for serving

I used to be suspicious of dolmas, a Mediterranean hors d'oeuvre made from rice stuffed into grape leaves. They often have a tinny smell and briny flavor that does nothing for me. When MaryAnn, one of my dearest friends, gave me one of her homemade dolmas to eat for the first time, I made sure to have water nearby with which to choke it down. But instead of gagging, I experienced a dolma revelation—the flavor was sweet-sour, not pickle-y, with pomegranate seeds and dill for color, crunch, and a lovely fresh flavor.

MaryAnn supplies herself with grape leaves often foraged from vines that grow alongside a Manhattan brownstone. But if you can't find them fresh, try to buy the Orlando brand of canned grape leaves. I planted grapevines on the farm just for MaryAnn—they didn't take, but I haven't stopped trying. My goal is to one day grow enough to always keep MaryAnn in constant supply of fresh leaves so that she doesn't have to steal them from homes anymore!

This recipe is also inspired by one from Jon Andrew Wolohojian, a dear friend who is no longer on this earth.

✳ ✳ ✳

Bring a medium pot of water to a boil. Add the rice and cook until it is just shy of al dente, about 10 minutes. Drain through a fine-mesh sieve and set aside.

Place the grape leaves on your worksurface. Using a paring knife, remove the stems from the leaves and then place the leaves in a large bowl of warm water to soak while you prepare the filling.

In a large bowl, mix the parboiled rice with the onions, pine nuts, raisins, lemon juice, canola oil, olive oil, sugar, salt, and pepper. Set aside.

Drain the leaves into a colander, and then transfer them to a large plate lined with paper towels or a kitchen towel. With another towel, pat the leaves dry. Place 25 leaves on your worksurface, ribbed-side up, stem end pointing toward you. Add 2 tbsp filling to each leaf, placing it just above the stem and gently arranging the filling so it spreads horizontally. Fold the sides of one leaf over the filling and then, while holding the sides, fold the stem end up and over the filling. Continue rolling the grape leaf somewhat loosely until you reach the end of the leaf. Set the stuffed grape leaf, seam-side down, in a large Dutch oven or other heavy pot. Repeat with the remaining leaves, fitting the first 25 dolmas into the Dutch oven or pot in a snug single layer. Fill and fold the remaining grape leaves, arranging the second batch of dolmas in a snug second layer directly on top of the first.

Cover the second layer with a flat plate that covers all the dolmas. Pour in enough cold water to cover the leaves, and bring to a boil over high heat. Reduce the heat to low, cover, and simmer for 40 minutes. Turn off the heat but leave the pot covered. Let the stuffed grape leaves rest in the covered pot for at least 4 and up to 8 hours at room temperature.

Use tongs to carefully transfer the dolmas to a platter (or to an airtight container; the dolmas can be refrigerated for up to 5 days). Sprinkle with pomegranate seeds and dill and serve.

THIN-CRUST PIZZA MARGHERITA

Makes 2 pizzas

FOR THE DOUGH

3 cups/385 g all-purpose flour, plus extra for kneading

2 tsp instant yeast

1 tbsp kosher salt

1½ tsp roughly ground black pepper

4 tbsp/60 ml extra-virgin olive oil

1 cup/240 ml lukewarm water

FOR THE PIZZAS

Semolina or cornmeal for the pizza peel

All-purpose flour for shaping crust

3 tbsp extra-virgin olive oil

1 cup/240 ml marinara, store-bought or homemade (page 53)

1 lb/455 g fresh mozzarella cheese, sliced into ¼-in-/6-mm-thick rounds

1⅓ cups/135 g finely grated Parmigiano-Reggiano cheese

¼ cup/10 g basil chiffonade (about 18 leaves, stacked, tightly rolled, and thinly sliced crosswise)

Pulling a bubbling-hot homemade pizza from the oven and transferring it from the pizza peel to a cutting board, where all my guests can ogle it, yields such great pleasure! I happily credit both Zoë François, author of the cookbook Artisan Bread in Five Minutes a Day, *and Mark Bittman, the* New York Times *columnist and* How to Cook Everything *author, for being the catalysts behind my expeditions in bread baking. Following their leads, I make the dough using a food processor, making it nearly foolproof. Sometimes I'll make the dough a day ahead and let it sit in the refrigerator overnight. The flavors develop, and the resulting crust is unbelievably light and crisp (and infinitely better than any pizza we have out here in the country). To keep the crust crunchy, I keep the toppings to a minimum— just a nice herb-loaded sauce and some good fresh mozzarella.*

✿ ✿ ✿

To make the dough: Place the flour, yeast, salt, and pepper in the bowl of a food processor and pulse to combine. Add 3 tbsp of the olive oil to the lukewarm water and, with the food processor running, begin adding the liquid in a slow, steady stream. Once all of the liquid is added, let the machine run until the dough forms a ball, 10 to 15 seconds. Grease a large bowl with the remaining 1 tbsp olive oil and set aside. Generously flour your worksurface and hands, and transfer the dough to the floured surface. Give the dough a few kneads just to bring it together, and transfer it to the oiled bowl. Cover the top of the bowl with a sheet of plastic wrap and set it aside in a warm and draft-free spot until it has doubled in size, about 2 hours.

Adjust an oven rack to the lowest position, place a pizza stone on the rack, and heat the oven to 500°F/260°C/gas 10.

Use your fingers to punch down the dough. Sprinkle some flour on your worksurface, and transfer the dough from the bowl to the floured surface. Divide the dough into two equal pieces and form each piece into a round ball. Cover the dough with another sheet of plastic wrap and let it rise for 30 minutes (at this point, the dough can be placed in an oiled bowl, covered with plastic wrap, and refrigerated overnight).

continued . . .

To make the pizzas: Cut out a piece of parchment paper that's about the same size as the surface of a pizza peel (or the flat underside of a baking sheet). Place it on the peel, sprinkle with semolina, and set aside. Place a small hill of flour on your worksurface, and set one piece of dough on top, turning the dough ball over in the flour to completely coat its surface. Gently toss the dough between your hands (or use a rolling pin) until it has flattened and widened into a 10-inch/25-cm circle. Place the dough on the pizza peel, and gently pull at its edges until it is stretched to about a 14- to 15-in/35.5- to 38-cm circle.

Use your fingers to spread 1 tbsp olive oil over the dough and then a rubber spatula to spread ½ cup/120 ml of the marinara. Top with half of the mozzarella, spreading it out evenly over the pizza's surface. Evenly sprinkle with ⅔ cup/65 g Parmigiano-Reggiano, drizzle 1½ tsp olive oil over the top, and finish with half of the basil leaves. Bake until the cheese is bubbly and browned, 8 to 12 minutes. Remove the pizza using the pizza peel, and transfer it to a cutting board. Wait 1 minute to allow the cheese to set up, then slice and serve immediately. Repeat with the remaining piece of dough and toppings.

RECIPE NOTE: NO STONE UNTURNED

When Charlie and I first saw our turmeric-colored two-story farmhouse, with its gray slate roof and pretty porch, we knew that this was the country home we were meant to own. While everything about the house was lovely, from the clawfoot tub in the downstairs bathroom to the herons that lingered around the pond in the morning, the one thing that needed immediate attention was the kitchen.

During our first spring there, we broke ground on our state-of-the-art kitchen, with top-notch appliances and every modern convenience you can think of. We used a blue-gray soapstone material for the counters and apron sink, and had a small piece left over. I eyed it, wondering if it would fit in the oven—and it did, almost as if it were made to fit on our Viking oven's shelf. It made an ideal pizza stone, yielding thin and shatteringly crispy-crusted pies, which have become a deliciously cheesy staple in our kitchen.

CHARLIE'S HERBY MARINARA

The end of spring is an exciting time at the farm. Not only are there baby goats frolicking and goslings hatching, but once the threat of frost is gone, it means we can move our herbs from their potted winter homes back outside and into the herb garden that lines the stone walkway up to our side door. Though we don't use a lot of herbs in our marinara sauce quantity-wise, by blooming the herbs' flavors in hot oil before adding canned tomatoes, we get an intensely bold herb flavor. This sauce, one of Charlie's specialties, is more robust than most traditional pizza sauces, allowing us to eke out big flavor in a pizza without weighing it down with a ton of cheese or meat. The marinara also makes a quick and wonderful pantry dinner when paired with good-quality pasta.

❈ ❈ ❈

Strip the leaves and needles off the oregano, rosemary, and thyme sprigs and place them in a medium saucepan. Add the olive oil, chiles, and pepper and cook over medium-high heat, stirring often, until the herb leaves have wilted and are beginning to become crisp, about 1½ minutes. Add the onion and salt and cook until the onion begins to soften, stirring often, about 3½ minutes.

Pour in the wine and scrape up any browned bits from the bottom of the pan. Once the wine and onion look somewhat jammy, about 3 minutes, stir in the tomatoes and bring the sauce to a boil. Reduce the heat to medium-low and simmer until the sauce is thick and chunky, stirring occasionally, about 15 minutes.

While the sauce is still warm, transfer it to a food mill and process it until smooth. Use immediately, or let cool and refrigerate up to 1 week, or freeze in a 1-qt/950-ml resealable plastic bag for up to 6 months.

Makes about 2½ cups/600 ml

1 large sprig fresh oregano

1 large sprig fresh rosemary

1 large sprig fresh thyme

3 tbsp extra-virgin olive oil

2 dried red chiles

½ tsp freshly ground black pepper

1 large red onion, finely chopped

2 tsp kosher salt

¼ cup/60 ml dry red wine (or ¼ cup/60 ml water plus 1 tbsp sugar)

3 cups/720 ml canned chopped tomatoes

SUMMERFIELD FARM'S
LAMB PASTRAMI

Serves 6

FOR THE BRINE

¼ lb/115 g kosher salt

8 cups/2 L ice water

1½ tbsp corn syrup

2 garlic cloves, finely minced

1½ tsp pickling spice

½ oz/15 g pink salt (TCM)
(see recipe note)

One 4-lb/1.8-kg boneless
lamb shoulder

FOR THE RUB

2 tbsp roughly cracked black
peppercorns

1 tbsp coriander seeds

1½ tsp cumin seeds

½ tsp juniper berries

FOR SMOKING

Hardwood charcoal briquettes

½ lb/225 g apple wood or alder
wood, soaked in water for 1 hour

FOR SERVING

Crusty bread

Grain mustard

The lamb that comes from Michael Katz's Summerfield Farm is supremely tender and beyond sweet—you won't find any trace of gaminess in this beyond-humanely raised lamb. It also happens to be the lamb that Clifton Booth, chef de cuisine at Max London's in Saratoga Springs, uses in his lamb pastrami. I would rather eat Clifton's pastrami, delicately cured and clean in flavor, over New York City beef pastrami any day. It is a bit of a process to make, requiring you to inject a brine into the lamb using a syringe (this greatly reduces the overall brining time—brining syringes can be found online) and brine the lamb, then cold-cure it with spices, then cold-smoke it, and finally hot-smoke it. The end result is so incredible, though, that it makes every minute of preparation worth it—once you try this, you'll never want for any other kind of pastrami. Clifton serves it with grilled bread and grain mustard, but Charlie and I love it served thinly sliced like salumi, with good, crusty bread on the side. A gas grill can be used in place of a charcoal grill.

❀ ❀ ❀

To make the brine: Whisk the salt with the ice water in a large pan (a roasting pan or deep oven roaster works well) until it is dissolved. Add the corn syrup, garlic, pickling spice, and pink salt and whisk to combine. Fill a meat syringe with some of the brine solution and inject the lamb with the brine in 2-in/5-cm intervals. Submerge the lamb in the remaining brine, cover with plastic wrap, and refrigerate for 3 days.

To make the rub: Pulse together the black peppercorns, coriander seeds, cumin seeds, and juniper berries in a coffee or spice grinder until roughly ground. Remove the lamb from the brine and place it on a worksurface. Dry the lamb with paper towels and then pat on the spice rub. Set a wire cooling rack over a rimmed baking sheet and place the lamb on top of the rack. Refrigerate it, uncovered, for 24 hours.

To smoke: Bank the briquettes to one side of the grill and build a medium-hot fire following the manufacturer's instructions. Place one-fourth of the soaked wood to one side of a 6-in-/15-cm-deep disposable aluminum pan. Poke about a dozen holes in the bottom of a 2-in-/5-cm-deep disposable aluminum pan and place it inside of the deeper one (the 2-in-/5-cm-deep pan should be 3 or 4 in/7.5 or 10 cm shorter than the 6-in-/15-cm-deep pan so that the wood is completely exposed and not covered by the perforated pan).

Set the pan on the lower grill grate (the grate that the charcoal is on). Once the wood starts to smoke, place the lamb in the perforated pan and cover the top of the perforated pan tightly with a sheet of heavy-duty aluminum foil (or a doubled sheet of regular aluminum foil). Turn up one corner to allow some of the heat to escape. Insert an instant-read thermometer into the open corner to ensure that the interior temperature of the covered pan remains between 80°F and 100°F/28°C and 38°C (to increase or decrease the temperature, add or remove briquettes as necessary to make the fire hotter or cooler). Cold-smoke the lamb for 3 hours, replenishing the wood and briquettes as necessary.

After 3 hours, close the aluminum flap and hot-smoke the lamb, keeping the interior temperature of the "smoker" between 160°F to 200°F/70°C and 95°C, replenishing the briquettes and wood as necessary, until the internal temperature of the lamb reads 150°F/65°C, about 1½ hours.

To serve: Take the lamb off the grill and let it rest for at least 30 minutes before thinly slicing it against the grain. The lamb can be served warm, at room temperature, or cold, thinly sliced with crusty bread and grain mustard.

RECIPE NOTE: TCM

Tinted curing mixture (TCM) is a combination of mostly table salt and about 6 percent sodium nitrate; it is used to cure meat and fish, giving pastrami and corned beef that trademark pink color (without it the meat would be a homely greenish gray—though it would still taste great). There are many online sources for it, or if you're on good terms with your local butcher (or know a restaurant that makes its own sausages or cures its own meats), you can ask to purchase a small quantity from him.

FARM ❋ YARN

THE COURTHOUSE COMMUNITY GARDEN

Part of what we love about living in the country is the relationship we have to the land. With all the open space there is out here, we recognize the great potential for utilizing farm land and pastures in a sustainable and positive way.

One of the projects that Charlie set his sights on was to bring a community garden to Salem, New York. He reached out to our friend—a local food writer, locavore, community activist, cooking teacher, and member of the school board (people do tend to wear many hats up in these parts!)— Annette Nielsen. They recruited five others, including Nancy Hand Higby, a local gardener and landscape designer, to help set a mission and goals for the garden. All the members agreed that the garden should benefit the local food pantry (a place that offers fresh and frozen locally grown vegetables to families in need), involve students from the community, and be managed by the kids who would, in turn, gain incredible life experiences, like learning how to run a business, engage others, develop work ethics, and hone their interpersonal skills.

Sheldon Brown, a partner of Woody Hill Farm, generously donated an eight-thousand-square-foot parcel of land conveniently located adjacent to both the school and the community center. Annette got the America the Beautiful Fund to donate seeds for flowers, herbs, and vegetables, and then other organizations followed suit, including A & J Agway, the National Peanut Board, and CaroVail, all of which committed resources like fertilizer, gardening tools, and preserving supplies, not to mention funding for the garden. It was amazing how everyone came together to make this little community garden (eight times the size of the White House kitchen garden) happen. Even our indispensable farm construction manager, Justin Rushinski, donated $500 to the cause!

Once they got the space, the funding, and the raw materials, it was time to start growing. The schoolchildren started seeds in recycled newspaper containers. Now nearly three hundred children are reaping the rewards from about eighty beds, harvesting gorgeous tomatoes, greens, lettuces, flowers, and even peanuts. With the garden in full swing, the children (some of whom get paid for their work) are learning first-hand about the science of gardening year-round. They sell produce at the farmers' market in the summer and winterize the beds in the fall. The little garden has become a source of great pride for the community. Most

of the produce gets donated to the
local food pantry; however, Charlie
is also working to coordinate the
Courthouse Community Garden's efforts
with the Lunch, Learn & Play program
(see page 79), the Battenkill Kitchen
(see page 134), and the Al Fresco
Weekend at the Salem Courthouse, a
yearly celebration feeding four hundred diners foods from local farms—
the community garden being one of them.
None of this would be possible without
community involvement, fundraising,
and the generosity of volunteers.

GINGER-SOY FRESH HAM
WITH ROASTED GARLIC

Serves 10

FOR THE SHICHIMI POWDER

6 dried red chiles

1 tbsp ground ginger

1 tbsp whole black peppercorns

1 tbsp whole pink peppercorns

1 tbsp coriander seeds

1 tbsp black sesame seeds

1 tbsp white sesame seeds

FOR THE BRINE

3 qt/3 L water

¾ cup/150 g kosher salt

¾ cup/150 g sugar

1 tbsp shichimi powder
(recipe above)

¼ cup/60 ml mirin (rice wine)

2 tbsp rice vinegar

2 tbsp soy sauce

When I'm not on the farm, I'm often traveling around the world, learning about other foodways, cultures, and ingredients, and speaking about Indian food. This particular recipe was influenced by a trip to Japan, during which Charlie and I became spellbound by the dedication and pride that chefs there devote to the dishes they prepare. They execute restraint and subtlety, allowing the quality of the ingredients to shine through the preparations. Returning inspired, I came up with this wonderfully delicious and comforting roast pork with the addition of Japanese ingredients such as shoyu (Japanese soy sauce), the Japanese seven-spice powder shichimi, and toasted sesame oil. Sometimes, when we really want to be decadent (and very un-Japanese!), instead of using butter and flour to thicken the gravy, I add crème fraîche and heavy cream instead. It is glorious!

Be sure to use only freshly ground black pepper in the sauce—it makes all the difference. I've included my American-country version of shichimi that I whip up when I run out of the real thing. You can find true Japanese shichimi powder (made with seaweed, Sichuan peppercorns, and other exotic spices) online at Korin.com. I rarely use stock in my cooking, but when I do, it's almost always made from a high-quality concentrate like the brands Aromont or More Than Gourmet, both available in some supermarkets and most specialty-food stores.

❋ ❋ ❋

To make the shichimi: Place the chiles, ginger, black peppercorns, pink peppercorns, coriander seeds, black sesame seeds, and white sesame seeds in a small frying pan and toast over medium heat, shaking the pan often, until the spices are fragrant, 1 to 2 minutes. Transfer the spices to a large plate to cool, and then pour them into a spice grinder and process until powdery. Shichimi can be stored in an airtight container in a cool, dry, and dark spot for up to 1 month.

To make the brine: Pour 1 qt/1 L of the water into a large bowl. Add the salt and sugar, whisking until dissolved. Pour the mixture into a large pot. Add the remaining 2 qt/2 L water, and then whisk in the shichimi powder, mirin, rice vinegar, and soy sauce.

Add the ham to the brine, cover with a lid or plastic wrap, and refrigerate for 2 hours.

Heat the oven to 325°F/165°C/gas 3. Whisk together the canola oil, ginger, soy sauce, mirin, sesame oil, and the 1½ tsp shichimi. Remove the ham from the brine and place it on a rimmed baking sheet. Blot it dry, and then smear the rub all over it. Set aside for 30 minutes.

Place the garlic and the mixed herbs in a deep, heavy-bottomed roasting pan. Set the ham on top, and place the pan in the oven until the ham reads 160°F/70°C on an instant-read thermometer, about 2½ hours.

Place the ham on a cutting board. Remove the roasted garlic from the pan and set aside (discard the herbs in the pan). Pour off and discard all but 2 tbsp of the fat in the roasting pan. In a small bowl, mash together the butter and flour and set aside. Heat the fat in the roasting pan over medium-high heat (you may have to place the pan over two burners), add the sherry, and scrape up any browned bits from the bottom of the pan. Stir in the broth and bring it to a simmer, then whisk in the butter paste until the mixture is smooth. Season with salt, and add the pepper and remaining 1 tbsp shichimi. Once a few bubbles burst at the top of the gravy, turn off the heat, and pour it into a gravy boat.

Carve the ham, and arrange it on a platter (make sure to include the cracklings). Scatter the garlic around the ham, and serve with gravy on the side.

One 8-lb/3.6-kg fresh ham scored in ¾- to 1-in/2- to 2.5-cm intervals in each direction to create a diamond pattern

⅓ cup/80 ml canola or grapeseed oil

3-in/7.5-cm piece fresh ginger, peeled and grated

3 tbsp soy sauce (preferably Japanese shoyu)

2 tsp mirin (rice wine)

1 tsp toasted sesame oil

1½ tsp shichimi powder, plus 1 tbsp (recipe at left)

3 heads garlic, top one third sliced off (so the tops of the cloves are exposed) and cloves separated

6 large sprigs fresh mixed herbs (such as lemon verbena, rosemary, summer savory, tarragon, or thyme)

2 tbsp unsalted butter, at room temperature

3 tbsp all-purpose flour

¼ cup/60 ml dry sherry

3 cups/720 ml cups beef broth

Kosher salt

3 tbsp freshly ground black pepper

BANANA-CARAMEL PUDDING

Serves 8 to 10

FOR THE PUDDING

3 large eggs

2 tsp vanilla paste or vanilla extract

1½ cups/360 ml milk

1½ cups/360 ml heavy cream

¾ cup/150 g sugar

⅛ tsp kosher salt

FOR THE CARAMEL SAUCE

½ cup/115 g unsalted butter

¾ cup/175 ml heavy cream

¾ tsp kosher salt

1 cup/200 g sugar

1 tbsp fresh lemon juice

FOR THE WHIPPED CREAM

2½ cups/600 ml heavy cream

½ cup/100 g sugar

1¼ tsp vanilla bean paste or
vanilla extract, or ⅓ vanilla bean

FOR ASSEMBLY

5 bananas

4 cups/360 g vanilla wafers

I don't know how it happened, but I've developed quite a fondness (and following) for my versions of Southern classics like fried chicken, biscuits, and even banana cream pie. Indian food is all about layers of flavor, so I approach these foods with the same agenda. In my version of banana pudding, I layer bananas with an incredibly rich vanilla crème pâtissier, *a slightly salty caramel sauce, generous spoonfuls of whipped cream, and the requisite vanilla wafers to create a trifle-like dessert that promises to get even the most Southern of Southerners drooling. I keep the caramel on the soft side so that, even after being refrigerated, it retains a somewhat saucy quality. It goes without saying to use the freshest eggs you can find for the pudding.*

❉ ❉ ❉

To make the pudding: Whisk the eggs with the vanilla in a large bowl and set aside. Bring the milk, heavy cream, sugar, and salt to a simmer in a large saucepan over medium-high heat. Turn off the heat and whisk a little of the hot liquid into the egg mixture. Continue adding more hot milk until the eggs are tempered and the bottom of the bowl is warm to the touch and then return the egg mixture to the saucepan with the remaining milk. Turn the heat to medium-high and cook, stirring constantly with a wooden spoon or whisk, until the pudding thickens and you can draw a clear line through the custard on the back of a spoon, about 5 minutes (don't let the custard boil—this will cause the eggs to curdle). Pour the custard through a medium sieve and into a medium bowl. Whisk to cool slightly, cover flush with plastic wrap, and refrigerate until it is completely cool, about 2 hours.

To make the caramel sauce: Microwave together the butter, heavy cream, and salt until the butter is melted (or melt the butter with the cream and salt in a small saucepan). Whisk to combine and set aside. Place the sugar and lemon juice in a medium saucepan. Melt the sugar over medium-high heat, swirling the pan occasionally to evenly distribute the heat, until the sugar is a deep nutty brown and smells bittersweet, 10 to 12 minutes. Pour in the butter mixture (be careful—the sauce will hiss and

continued . . .

bubble up) and then place the mixture back over medium-high heat to return it to a boil. Turn off the heat and set the saucepan aside to let the caramel cool to room temperature, 1 to 2 hours.

To make the whipped cream: Place the heavy cream, sugar, and vanilla (if using a vanilla bean, split the pod and scrape out the seeds, adding them to the cream; save the pod and place it in a jar of sugar to infuse it with vanilla flavor) in the bowl of a stand mixer (or large bowl if using a hand mixer) and whip it on medium speed until it is frothy. Increase the speed to medium-high and whip until you get stiff peaks. Refrigerate until you're ready to assemble the pudding.

To assemble: Peel and thinly slice the bananas and set aside (wait to slice the bananas until you're ready to assemble the dish, otherwise, they'll brown). Evenly spread 1 cup whipped cream over the bottom of a large trifle dish or punch bowl. Top with a layer of bananas and 1 cup/240 ml pudding. Place about 20 vanilla wafers in a flat layer on top of the pudding and evenly drizzle ½ cup/120 ml caramel over the wafers. Repeat the layering process three times, beginning with the whipped cream, followed by some sliced bananas, pudding, wafers, and caramel. Finish the pudding with a final layer of whipped cream (you should have about 1 cup remaining after repeating four layers), cover with plastic wrap, and refrigerate for at least 6 hours or overnight. Serve in dessert bowls.

SPICED RHUBARB JAM

Rhubarb grows like weeds around here, and come late May, all the neighbors are desperate to give away what they have. It didn't take me long to figure out that the best way to use up our rhubarb was to turn it into a jam, officially kicking off the preserving season of the spring, summer, and fall. My rhubarb jam is savory like a chutney, thick like a relish, and sweet like a jam. I add spices such as peppercorns and saffron for an unusually deep and haunting flavor. Currants give it some texture, and dried rose petals and fresh lemon juice and rind make it perfumed and alluring.

It's heavenly with Grandma Mae's Biscuits (page 77) and crème fraîche. One neighbor, Betty Osborne, uses it as a glaze for her baked chicken, and I've used it to glaze a country ham. My mother even took a few jars to India, where she smears it on toast for breakfast. For a country-size batch that yields 18 to 20 pt/7.5 to 9.5 L of jam, quadruple the recipe and use a very large 15-qt/14.2-L pot.

✽ ✽ ✽

Toast the saffron and ¼ tsp of the salt in a small frying pan over medium heat until fragrant, 30 seconds to 1 minute. Transfer to a mortar and pestle (or small bowl) and grind into a fine powder (if using a bowl, pulverize the saffron using the back of a spoon).

Place the rhubarb, apples, sugar, lemon juice and rind, currants, minced ginger, rose petals, peppercorns, ground ginger, ground saffron, and remaining ¾ tsp salt in a large nonreactive pot. Bring to a boil over medium heat, stirring often, and cook until thick and jammy, 30 to 45 minutes. Turn off the heat and immediately process according to the instructions on page 111.

Makes 4 pt/2 L

¼ tsp saffron threads

1 tsp kosher salt

4 lb/1.8 kg rhubarb, ends trimmed and stalks thinly sliced

3 crisp apples, halved, cored, and thinly sliced

2½ lb/1.2 kg sugar

Juice and rind from 1 lemon, rind sliced into thin strips

½ cup/85 g currants

1½-in/4-cm piece ginger, peeled and finely minced

2 tbsp dried rose petals

½ tsp freshly ground pink peppercorns

¼ tsp ground ginger

RHUBARB AND
RASPBERRY COBBLER WITH
CRÈME FRAÎCHE CREAM

Serves 8

FOR THE RHUBARB

3 lb/1.4 kg rhubarb, ends trimmed and stalks sliced 1 in/2.5 cm thick

1 cup/125 g raspberries

1 cup/200 g sugar

Zest of 1 orange

FOR THE TOPPING

1½ cups/175 g all-purpose flour

¼ cup/50 g sugar

1½ tsp baking powder

¼ tsp kosher salt

¾ cup/175 ml buttermilk

4 tbsp/55 g unsalted butter, melted

1 large egg

FOR THE CRÈME FRAÎCHE CREAM

½ cup/120 ml heavy cream

1½ tbsp sugar

½ cup/120 ml crème fraîche, store-bought or homemade (page 214)

The idea for this cobbler was inspired by one we shared with U.S. Congressman Scott Murphy and his scholarly wife, Jennifer Hogan, who are known for hosting epic brunches at their Glens Falls home. After enjoying her rhubarb cobbler at one early-summer Sunday gathering, I knew I had to make it a part of my repertoire. I added a handful of supersweet garnet raspberries from Meg Southerland's crop over at Gardenworks, our favorite nursery and country store, to boost the color and lend a natural sweetness to the tart rhubarb. I love the cobbler with a heaping cloud of tangy whipped crème fraîche on top, but Charlie is satisfied by simply pouring milk over the cobbler. If you're from the South, you might agree.

❀ ❀ ❀

Adjust one oven rack to the lower-middle position and another oven rack to the lowest position. Preheat the oven to 375°F/190°C/gas 5. Line a rimmed baking sheet with aluminum foil and set aside.

To prepare the rhubarb: Place the rhubarb, raspberries, sugar, and orange zest in a large pot over low heat. Cover the pot and cook, stirring occasionally, until the rhubarb is tender and the mixture is very juicy, 15 to 20 minutes.

Using a slotted spoon, transfer the cooked fruit to a 2-in-/5-cm-deep 2-qt/1.9-L baking dish and set aside. Bring the fruit juices in the pot to a simmer over medium heat and cook until the volume is reduced by half and the consistency becomes thick and jammy, 8 to 10 minutes. Use a rubber spatula to scrape the liquid over the fruit in the baking dish, and set aside.

To make the topping: Sift together the flour, sugar, baking powder, and salt in a medium bowl. In a large bowl, whisk together the buttermilk, butter, and egg. Add the flour mixture to the buttermilk mixture and, using a wooden spoon, gently stir the two together until the batter is lumpy with a few remaining dry streaks. Using a rubber spatula, scrape the batter over the fruit in the baking dish so that it evenly covers the surface.

Place the aluminum foil–lined baking sheet on the lowest oven rack and the cobbler on the lower-middle rack (the foil-lined baking sheet will catch the juices that bubble out of the baking dish). Bake until the fruit juices bubble around the sides of the cobbler, the topping is golden brown, and a cake tester inserted into the topping comes out clean, about 45 minutes. Remove the baking dish from the oven and set it aside to cool. Remove the aluminum foil–lined baking sheet from the oven.

To make the crème fraîche cream: In the bowl of a stand mixer (or in a large bowl if using a hand mixer), beat together the cream and sugar until soft peaks are formed. Add the crème fraîche and continue to beat until medium-stiff peaks form.

Serve the cobbler hot, warm, or at room temperature and topped with the crème fraîche cream.

VARIATION: INDIVIDUAL COBBLERS
Divide the fruit filling among eight 1-cup/240-ml ramekins. Top with the cobbler topping, and place the ramekins on a rimmed baking sheet. Bake until the fruit is bubbling around the edges, the topping is golden brown, and a cake tester inserted into the center of the topping comes out clean, 20 to 25 minutes. Remove the baking sheet from the oven and set the ramekins aside to cool slightly before serving.

VARIATION: CARAMELY CRÈME FRAÎCHE CREAM
Bring the cream and 1½ tbsp light or dark brown sugar to a simmer in a small saucepan over medium heat, stirring often to dissolve the sugar. Turn off the heat, and pour the sweetened cream into a small bowl. Cover with plastic wrap, and refrigerate until the cream is chilled, about 2 hours. Proceed in making the crème fraîche cream as described.

ALMOST-FLOURLESS CARAMEL-LACQUERED CHOCOLATE-PEANUT TORTE

Serves 8

11 tbsp/165 g unsalted butter at room temperature

1 slice 2- to 3-day-old bread (or 1 fresh slice toasted in a warm oven until dry but not browned)

1 cup/150 g roasted and salted peanuts

2½ tbsp dark-roasted peanut flour (see Farmhouse Resources page 222)

½ cup/100 g packed dark brown sugar

4 large eggs, separated

2 tsp vanilla bean paste or vanilla extract

½ cup/130 g granulated sugar, plus 3 tbsp

4 oz/60 g chocolate (70 to 80 percent cacao), grated

Peanuts are very country, very old-fashioned, and very American—and I love them—especially with chocolate. This torte is a cross between a brownie and a chocolate cake that is topped with a crème brûlée–style crackled sugar crust. It's wonderfully decadent. The ground peanuts and peanut flour really give the chocolate a warmth and nuttiness that is at once alluring, comforting, and really delicious. It's an "almost" flourless chocolate cake because I include a slice of several-day-old bread in the batter. This addition can easily be eliminated for those with gluten sensi- tivities or if making this cake for Passover, when only flourless dishes can grace the table. You can vary this cake by using almonds or walnuts in place of the peanuts if you like, but we like peanuts and that certain bit of country charm they seem to bring to the table, even though the cake looks as chic as can be.

❁ ❁ ❁

Preheat the oven to 325°F/165°C/gas 3. Grease a 9-in/23-cm spring- form pan with 1 tbsp of the butter. Place the pan on top of a sheet of parchment paper, and trace a circle around the pan; cut it out and place the paper circle in the bottom of the pan to grease the underside. Flip the paper circle over and press it into place. Set aside.

Place the bread in a food processor and pulse until it forms medium- coarse crumbs. Add the peanuts and peanut flour, and pulse until the texture is like rough sand (don't overprocess the mixture, or it will become peanut butter).

continued . . .

Using a stand mixer fitted with the paddle attachment or a hand mixer and a large bowl, cream the remaining 10 tbsp/155 g butter until it is fluffy and pale. Add the brown sugar and continue to cream until pale, then add the egg yolks, one at a time, mixing thoroughly between additions and scraping the bottom and sides of the bowl as needed. Add the vanilla, reduce the speed to low, and add the peanut mixture.

In another bowl, whisk the egg whites with the 3 tbsp sugar until the whites form stiff peaks. Fold the whipped whites into the batter in three additions, adding the grated chocolate along with the last addition, folding until just a few streaks of white remain. Scrape the mixture into the prepared cake pan and bake until the sides pull away from the edges of the pan and a cake tester inserted into the center of the cake comes out clean, about 1 hour.

Remove the pan from the oven and set on a wire cooling rack for 5 minutes before releasing the latch and lifting the side of the pan away from the bottom. Let cool completely before inverting the cake onto a large flat plate, cutting board, or baking sheet, lifting off the pan bottom, and peeling away the parchment circle. Reinvert the cake onto a cake plate or platter.

Place the remaining ½ cup/100 g sugar and ⅔ cup/160 ml cold water into a small saucepan. Cook over medium heat, stirring until the sugar dissolves, and then let the sugar simmer, swirling the pan occasionally, until the liquid becomes an amber-color caramel, 15 to 17 minutes. Remove from the heat immediately and, using an offset spatula, pour and spread the caramel syrup over the top of the cake. Let the cake cool, then slice and serve at room temperature.

RECIPE NOTE: THE PEANUT GANG

In this recipe, I replace the customary almonds, hazelnuts, or walnuts with the unexpected peanut. Humble and pleasing, the peanut isn't a nut at all but rather a legume. It's rich in protein and fiber and is considered brain food because of its high nutritive value. Since they are so nutritious, readily available, and kind on the wallet, we go through loads of peanuts at the farm—whole peanuts in Peanut Chaat (page 126), ground peanuts in the Chocolate-Peanut Tart with Caramel and Chocolate Mousse (page 209), and finally peanut flour in my recipe for Peanut Fried Chicken (page 133). We even help grow them at the Courthouse Community Garden (see page 56) in Salem.

There are four basic varieties of American peanut: Spanish, Runner, Valencia, and Virginia. Spanish peanuts are the smallest and are most often used in candies; Runners are a popular choice for peanut butter; Sweet Valencias are delicious boiled; and, my favorite, Virginia peanuts are the largest and most delicious, especially for cooking. When purchasing peanuts, be sure to check the label and look for the place of origin—many peanut-growing countries buy American seeds, grow them abroad, and then sell them as "Virginia" peanuts. If you can't locate true Virginia peanuts, check online sources like Royal Oak Peanuts (see page 227)—believe me, they're worth it.

CHAPTER TWO

SUMMER

❋

Sweet Corn, Snap Peas, and

a Steady Stream of New Faces

Short, sweet, and snappy: This is summertime in North Country. Almost before we realize that we are in the midst of summer, it's gone. So while it's here, we enjoy ourselves to the fullest.

For the most part, the weather is so pleasant and lovely that all we need are a few fans going during the daytime. On those rare hot and humid days that make their way up north to us, I make chilled herbal tea using lemon thyme, lemon verbena, or mint steeped in boiling water, chilled, and sweetened with sugar syrup.

At night, the fresh country air invades the house, bringing a slight chill into the sitting room on even the stickiest days. Curling up on the sofa with a light blanket isn't out of the question. When the temperature drops, the mist rolls in from the hills in thick waves, settling on the land around the pond at the back of the house. As I wash the dinner dishes, the sounds of honking geese and echoing frogs draw my gaze to the window, and I try in vain to locate them through the thick curtain of blue fog.

Living at the farm during the summer is truly a gift. We get the juiciest and most perfumed strawberries, unbelievable corn, potatoes of all colors and shapes, sweeter-than-sugar sugar snap peas, amazing tomatoes, and a cornucopia of herbs, beans, and all kinds of vegetables that enchant with  their robustness. North Country simply shines in the summertime. Sometimes it seems like all we have to do is toss a seed into the earth, and the rich soil, weekly rain, ample sunshine, and tempered evenings make it blossom and flourish.

Summer happens to be the time when everyone in the country has friends and family visiting, and our home is no exception. Our door never stops revolving as the farm becomes an extension of Manhattan, New Delhi, and all points in between. At the farm, we hold steadfast to one rule: You are always welcome, as long as you're willing to be part of the family. We don't expect anyone to stand on formality—what's ours is yours. We ask our friends to treat our kitchen, garden, and home as if it were their own.

For those who can't seem to sit still for more than a few minutes, peace and solitude is found in pitching in to weed the herb and vegetable gardens, while others help us feed the animals, make trips to the farmstand or the supermarket, or entertain us with jokes, stories, and gossip. On some busy weekends, we have one group of guests leaving after breakfast, with the next entourage arriving in the early afternoon—Charlie has to be very quick about changing the sheets! Between locals dropping by with fresh river trout or homemade jam, and visitors calling on us from all corners of the world, each day becomes a packed whirlwind of cooking, eating, gabbing, and sightseeing. Through a good mix of people, lots of wonderful energy, and tons of peak produce, we celebrate these weeks to their fullest.

While this action-packed season offers Charlie and me little time for rest and relaxation, if it weren't for visitors, we'd probably be lonely up here at the farm, since most of our local farmer-friends vanish completely, busy with feeding, tending, and milking their animals; baling hay; harvesting vegetables; and making cheese. Aside from a friendly stop-by or the rare occasion when we lure them to our dining table with a promise of fried *pakoras* or homemade strawberry ice cream, we know that we'll rekindle our local friendships during the late autumn and winter, when the sun's rays are less potent, the land grows still, and time becomes the commodity of the season.

DEVILED EGGS WITH
CILANTRO, CHILES, AND SPICES

Makes 2 dozen deviled eggs

12 hard-boiled eggs, peeled and halved lengthwise

2 tbsp peanut or canola oil

30 fresh or 45 frozen curry leaves (see page 215), finely chopped

1 tsp brown mustard seeds

¾ tsp cumin seeds

1 small red onion, finely chopped

1½ tsp kosher salt

1 small jalapeño (seeded and ribbed for less heat), finely chopped

1 tbsp Sambhaar Powder (page 219)

½ cup/120 ml crème fraîche, store-bought or homemade (page 214)

¼ cup/60 ml mayonnaise, store-bought or homemade (page 217)

¼ cup/60 ml fresh lemon juice

½ cup/20 g finely chopped fresh cilantro

This spiced twist on classic deviled eggs relies on fresh chiles, fresh cilantro, and sambhaar *powder for heat, flavor, and color and on crème fraîche and lemon juice for an incredibly rich tang. If you have access to farm-fresh eggs, I encourage you to use them, though do refrigerate them for at least seven days before boiling. Aging allows the inner membrane between the shell and the white to loosen, making the cooked eggs easier to peel. I promise that the richness of the yolks and their intense yellow color make them completely worth it.*

❀ ❀ ❀

Pop the yolks out of the halved eggs, place them in a medium bowl, and set aside. Place the halved egg whites on a platter, cover with plastic wrap, and refrigerate until you're ready to fill them.

Heat the oil, curry leaves, mustard seeds, and cumin seeds in a large frying pan over medium-high heat, stirring often, until the curry leaves are fragrant and the mustard seeds begin to pop, 1½ to 2 minutes. Add the onion and salt and cook, stirring often, until the onion is browned around the edges, about 5 minutes. Pour in 2 tbsp water and continue to cook until the onion is very dark brown, about 2 minutes, then stir in another ¼ cup/60 ml water, stirring and scraping any browned bits off the bottom of the pan. Stir in the jalapeño and *sambhaar* powder, and cook until the mixture begins to stick to the bottom of the pan, about 30 seconds, stirring often. Scrape the mixture into the bowl with the egg yolks.

Using a fork or potato masher, mash the yolks and onion-spice mixture together until very smooth. Stir in the crème fraîche and mayonnaise and, once they're incorporated, mix in the lemon juice and cilantro. Taste for seasoning and then cover with plastic wrap and chill for at least 1 hour or up to overnight before filling the egg whites. Once the mixture has set up, spoon or pipe (using a pastry bag fitted with a round tip) a generous amount into each egg white half (I usually use a generous 1 tbsp of filling for each egg white half). Once the eggs are filled, either serve immediately or cover with plastic wrap and chill up to overnight before serving.

SCRAMBLED EGGS WITH TOMATOES, ONIONS, AND HERBS

A good friend of ours, Sal Rizzo, the owner of the De Gustibus cooking school at Macy's in New York City, came to visit one summer and made this dish for Charlie and me using ripe tomatoes and fresh basil from the garden. The dish immediately charmed everyone at the table—scrambled eggs with personality! Even people who say they don't like scrambled eggs love these. They're bursting with fresh flavor and richness, especially when made with just-collected eggs from our henhouse. For a fantastic country marinara for pasta, just leave out the eggs.

❀ ❀ ❀

Place the butter and pepper in a large pot over medium heat. Once the butter is melted, add the oregano and cook, stirring often, for 30 seconds. Add the onion and jalapeño (if using) and cook, stirring occasionally, until the onion softens, about 5 minutes. Stir in the tomatoes and 1 tsp of the salt and cook until the mixture is somewhat dry looking, stirring occasionally, about 6 minutes.

Meanwhile, whisk together the eggs and remaining ¾ tsp salt in a large bowl. Reduce the heat of the tomato mixture to medium-low and add the eggs to the pot in a slow and steady stream, stirring the mixture constantly until all the beaten eggs are added. Continue to cook while stirring until the eggs begin to stick to the bottom of the pan, about 5 minutes. They will be a very soft-set scramble. Stir in the basil and serve immediately.

Serves 6 to 8

6 tbsp/85 g unsalted butter

½ tsp freshly ground black pepper

6 fresh oregano leaves, finely chopped

1 large red onion, finely chopped

1 jalapeño, finely chopped (seeded and ribbed for less heat), or ¼ tsp red pepper flakes (optional)

3 large tomatoes, cored and chopped

1¾ tsp kosher salt

16 large eggs

10 fresh basil leaves, finely chopped

GRANDMA MAE'S BISCUITS

*Once you have eaten these biscuits, there is no turning back. You will
be hooked and spoiled for life, as I was, when my very dear friend Brett
Bannon served them during a stay at our farm. Brett and his partner,
Jon, are my saviors when I'm in Minneapolis, shuttling me to and from
the airport and cooking classes that I'm teaching, taking me to wonderful
restaurants, introducing me to friends in the community, and, above all
else, welcoming me as a guest in their home. One morning, Charlie and I
awoke to these biscuits, hot from the oven, pillowy tender, and as flaky and
delicious as you can imagine. The recipe comes from Brett's mother, who
learned how to make them from her mother, Mae Norris of Jacksonville,
Florida. Brett grew up eating these biscuits every morning, waking up
not to an alarm clock but to the clinking of a knife working the butter into
the flour. I've adopted the breakfast tradition at our farm and thank him,
his mother, and Grandma Mae, of course, for this beautifully simple and
incredibly delicious best-ever biscuit recipe. Leaf lard is the very best ren-
dered and clarified pork fat you can buy and makes these biscuits light and
fluffy. If you can't find it, use lard, or substitute all butter as indicated in
the ingredients.*

❊ ❊ ❊

Preheat the oven to 400°F/200°C/gas 6. Place 3 cups/385 g of the flour
in a large bowl. Chop ½ cup/115 g of the butter into ¼-in/6-mm, pieces
and add it to the flour along with the leaf lard (or additional 5 tbsp/75 g
salted butter if not using leaf lard). Use a pastry cutter to work the fat
into the flour until the mixture looks like cornmeal with pieces no larger
than a small pea.

Pour half of the cream into the dry ingredients, using a butter knife
to gently cut it into the dough. Add more cream, 2 tbsp at a time, until
there are no more dry spots remaining (you may end up with a bit of
liquid left over, depending on the humidity and the age of the flour).

Melt ¼ cup/55 g of the salted butter in a 10-in/25-cm cast-iron frying
pan over low heat. Turn off the heat and set aside.

continued . . .

Makes 11 or 12 biscuits

3½ cups/450 g self-rising flour

1 cup/225 g salted butter plus
5 tbsp/70 g leaf lard; or 1¼ cups
plus 1 tbsp/300 g salted butter

1¼ cups/300 ml heavy cream, plain
yogurt, milk, buttermilk, or any
combination thereof

Good butter (like Vermont
Butter and Cheese or Kerrygold),
for serving

Crème fraîche, store-bought or
homemade (page 214), for serving

Seasonal jam, store-bought or
homemade (page 109), for serving

Melt the remaining ¼ cup/55 g salted butter in a microwave-safe bowl and set aside. Place the remaining ½ cup/65 g flour in a medium bowl. Break the dough into 11 or 12 golf ball–size portions, dust with flour, and gently flatten between your palms as if they were snowballs. Dip the top of each slightly flattened biscuit (mine end up in a somewhat hexagon shape) into the melted butter in the bowl and place in the frying pan. Place the biscuits close together so the sides are touching (don't worry—they separate perfectly once they come out of the oven). If there is any melted butter left over in the bowl, drizzle it over the biscuits.

Bake until the biscuits are golden brown and nearly doubled in size, 20 to 25 minutes. Remove from the oven and set aside for 5 minutes before using a cake server to remove the biscuits from the pan (the first one is a bit tricky to unwedge, but the rest pop out easily). Serve immediately, while hot, with plenty of good butter, crème frâiche, and jam.

VARIATION: BISCUIT ADDENDUMS

Grandma Mae's original recipe calls for self-rising flour, but I get very close using all-purpose flour to which I add 1½ tbsp baking powder and ¾ tsp salt. On rare occasions when I crave a sweet biscuit, I'll add 2 tbsp sugar and the zest of 1 lemon to the dry ingredients. To turn the biscuits into a more savory indulgence, I add 1 tsp *ajwain* seeds (also called carom seeds) and ⅛ tsp cayenne pepper to the dry ingredients. Finally, if you are using sweet butter and not salted, add an additional ¼ tsp kosher salt to your dry ingredients.

FARM ✦ YARN

TEACHING KIDS TO EAT WELL

When we heard that proponents of the Salem Community Center wanted to include children from different towns and villages for the Lunch, Learn & Play Program, Charlie and I knew that we needed help.

It's a sad fact that the school lunch offered during the academic year is often the most nutritious hot meal a child receives during the day. So when school isn't in session—like during the summertime—children don't receive those balanced and healthful lunches. Extending the Lunch, Learn & Play Program to the summer so children could continue to receive healthful and free lunches five days a week—even during school breaks—just made sense.

Through lots of hard work and fundraising, the Lunch, Learn & Play Program was extended to July and August, Monday through Friday. Best yet, kids may go to the Courthouse Community Center not just for lunch, but also for a full day of learning and doing. Arts and crafts, working in the Courthouse Community Garden (see page 56), helping out in the local library, playing board games, participating in cooking demonstrations, and even growing peanuts are just some of the activities offered through this completely free program, funded entirely via private and corporate donations.

The program now serves up to one hundred children, mostly in kindergarten through third grade, getting them thinking about art, science, and, of course, food. In addition to helping out in the community garden, the kids often cook their own lunches at the Battenkill Kitchen (see page 134). Through food demos and hands-on classes, the children are taught how easy it is to cook from scratch—and how good a home-cooked meal made from fresh produce tastes. To bring the lesson home, the kids are encouraged to enter a community-wide recipe contest, in which the children submit one of their family's best recipes.

It's wonderful to see the whole community coming together and getting involved. Everyone works alongside one another to make sure that the children have fun. The expanded lunch hours and the programming made all the difference: We saw enrollment increase drastically, and we hope that the program continues to get bigger and better every year.

COUNTRY SALAD WITH
FIVE VINAIGRETTE VARIATIONS

Serves 8

8 cups/440 g tender leafy greens, washed and roughly torn if large

⅔ cup/150 ml vinaigrette or dressing (recipes follow)

Charlie is the designated salad maker at the house, and his simple salad creations are a customary addition to lunches, dinners, and even breakfast. We love the tender organic greens we get from Seth and Martha at Slack Hollow Farm—they have so much flavor and vibrancy that all they need is a drizzle of fresh-made vinaigrette to make a superb salad. Of course, you can add other ingredients, like shaved pickled red onions, halved cherry tomatoes, sliced apples, toasted nuts, dried fruit (blueberries, cherries, and strawberries are our favorites), grated Parmigiano-Reggiano, fresh chèvre, or bread toasted with olive oil and herbs. But sometimes a bowl of pristine greens simply dressed is all you need to make a statement.

Our pantry provides the inspiration for making vinaigrettes. There we find ingredients that can be as interesting as the other flavors in the meal. Tamarind Chutney (page 219), spicy Sriracha sauce, Dijon mustard, fresh ginger, and shoyu are all items we often have on hand that can lend uniqueness and vibrancy to a standard oil and acid vinaigrette. Charlie is great at ensuring that the dressing is interesting yet balanced—a play of sour, salty, sweet, bitter, and spicy tastes that, just like the underlying philosophy of Indian cookery, are as much about harmonious cohabitation as they are about singular nuance and personality. For us, salad is not about sacrifice, but is a celebration of clean flavors and simple executions.

❁ ❁ ❁

Place the greens in a large bowl. Just before serving, toss with the vinaigrette or dressing of your choice and serve.

GINGER AND SHOYU VINAIGRETTE

Makes about ¾ cup/180 ml

2-in/5-cm piece fresh ginger, peeled

2 tbsp honey

3 tbsp extra-virgin olive oil

3 tbsp fresh lemon juice

2 tbsp good-quality shoyu (Japanse soy sauce)

1 tbsp grain mustard

1 small shallot, roughly chopped

Grate the ginger using a microplane or ginger grater. Collect the grated
ginger in a soup spoon, hold it over a blender jar, and press on it with
your fingers to extract the juice. Add the honey, olive oil, lemon juice,
shoyu, mustard, and shallot. Purée in the blender until completely
smooth. Use immediately, or transfer to an airtight container and refrigerate for up to 2 days. (Note that the shallot's flavor will become stronger,
and the ginger's will become weaker, the longer the vinaigrette is kept in
the refrigerator.)

❀ ❀ ❀

NORTH COUNTRY BALSAMIC VINAIGRETTE

Makes about 1 cup/240 ml

3 tbsp balsamic vinegar

2 tbsp Dijon mustard

¼ tsp Herbes de Hebron (page 215) or herbes de Provence

½ tsp kosher salt

¼ tsp freshly ground black pepper

1 shallot or ½ small red onion, roughly chopped

1 garlic clove

½ tsp fresh oregano leaves or ¼ tsp dried oregano

½ tsp fresh rosemary leaves or ¼ tsp dried rosemary

¾ cup/180 ml exta-virgin olive oil

continued . . .

Whisk together the vinegar, mustard, Herbes de Hebron, salt, and pepper in a liquid measuring cup and set aside. Place the shallot, garlic, oregano, and rosemary in a food processor and process until fine. With the machine running, add the vinegar-herb mixture and process until smooth, then slowly begin to drizzle in the olive oil. Stop processing once all of the oil has been added and the vinaigrette is emulsified. Use immediately or transfer to an airtight container and refrigerate for up to 1 week. (Note that the shallot and garlic flavors will become stronger the longer the vinaigrette is kept in the refrigerator.)

❀ ❀ ❀

SUMMER TISANE VINAIGRETTE

Makes about ⅔ cup/165 ml

3 fennel fronds

2 dill fronds

1 sprig fresh basil (preferably variegated)

1 sprig fresh lavender

1 sprig fresh marjoram

4 fresh lemon verbena leaves

Juice of 2 lemons

¼ cup/60 ml tea oil

2 tbsp maple syrup (preferably medium-amber)

⅛ tsp cayenne pepper

⅛ tsp sea salt

¼ tsp freshly ground mixed or black pepper

Pick the leaves off the fennel, dill, basil, lavender, and marjoram and finely chop along with the lemon verbana leaves. Transfer the herbs to a small bowl and whisk in the lemon juice, tea oil, maple syrup, cayenne, salt, and pepper. Serve immediately or transfer to an airtight container and refrigerate for up to 1 day.

TANGY BUTTERMILK-TARRAGON DRESSING

Makes 1¼ cups/300 ml

½ cup/120 ml full-fat buttermilk (like Kate's Creamery)

½ cup/120 ml crème fraîche, store-bought or homemade (page 214)

Zest of 1 lemon, plus 1½ tbsp fresh lemon juice

¼ tsp sugar

½ tsp sea salt

1 tsp freshly ground black pepper

2 tbsp finely chopped fresh tarragon

1 tbsp finely chopped fresh chives

1 tbsp finely chopped fresh lemon thyme

Whisk together the buttermilk, crème fraîche, lemon zest and juice, sugar, salt, and pepper in a medium bowl. Add the tarragon, chives, and thyme and whisk to combine. Serve immediately or cover with plastic wrap and refrigerate overnight.

❊ ❊ ❊

SOUTHEAST ASIAN DRESSING

Makes 1 cup/240 ml

½ cup/120 ml Tamarind Chutney (page 219)

¼ cup/60 ml extra-virgin olive oil

Juice of 1 lime

½ tsp Sriracha hot sauce

¼ tsp sea salt

½ tsp freshly ground black pepper

¼ cup/10 g finely chopped fresh cilantro

7 fresh Thai basil leaves, very finely chopped

6 fresh mint leaves, stacked, rolled, and thinly sliced crosswise

1 Thai green chile, finely chopped (optional)

Whisk together the chutney, olive oil, lime juice, hot sauce, salt, and pepper in a medium bowl. Add the cilantro, basil, mint, and chile (if using) and whisk to combine. Use immediately or cover and refrigerate for up to 3 days.

Cabbage Slaw with Fresh Herbs and Peanuts

Serves 6 to 8

A ¾-in piece fresh ginger, peeled and grated

Juice of ½ lime

1½ tsp citrus vinegar or white wine vinegar

1½ tsp sugar

¾ tsp *chaat* masala (see page 214)

¼ tsp Toasted Cumin (page 221)

Pinch of cayenne pepper

2 tsp kosher salt

¼ tsp ground peppercorns

9 scallions, thinly sliced

1 jalapeño (seeded and veined for less heat), finely chopped (optional)

1 pint cherry or grape tomatoes, halved

½ cup finely chopped fresh cilantro

2 tbsp finely chopped fresh mint leaves

½ head green cabbage, halved, cored and finely sliced

¾ cup chopped roasted peanuts

Made with absolutely no oil or mayonnaise, we make this tangy-spicy-crunchy-herby slaw year-round, but it's especially great as a picnic salad in the summertime. It's quite nice with heavy summer fare like fried chicken and barbecue.

❀ ❀ ❀

In a large bowl, whisk together the ginger, lime juice, vinegar, sugar, *chaat* masala, toasted cumin, cayenne, salt, and peppercorns. Add the scallions, jalapeño, tomatoes, cilantro, and mint leaves and toss to combine. Add the cabbage and toss with your hands, making sure to coat it thoroughly with the other ingredients. Sprinkle with the peanuts and serve immediately, or cover with plastic wrap and refrigerate for up to 4 hours, sprinkling with the peanut just before serving.

CHUNKY
EGGPLANT DIP

One summer night, Stuart Ziehm, a local dairy farmer, and his fiancée, Jennifer, stopped by. Neither could say whether they were fans of eggplant before sampling the dip, but about fifteen minutes after I set it on the counter with toasted pita triangles, half of it was gone! It's so cooling, refreshing, and healthful that this dip doesn't just taste good to eat, it feels good to eat, too. I usually char the eggplant right on my gas stovetop. It does make a bit of a mess, though, so feel free to cook the eggplant on a gas or charcoal grill instead.

❈ ❈ ❈

Place a whole eggplant on a gas burner, and set the flame to medium-high. Char the eggplant, using tongs to turn it often (I turn it every 2 minutes or so), until the skin is completely black and papery and the eggplant is deflated, about 10 minutes total. Transfer it to a plate and cover with plastic wrap. Set aside until the eggplant is cool enough to handle, then halve it, scoop out the pulp, roughly chop it, and place it in a large bowl. Repeat with the second eggplant.

Add the onion, tomato, jalapeño, and olive oil to the bowl and gently stir to combine. In a medium bowl, whisk together the yogurt, cilantro, lemon juice, Aleppo pepper, sumac, salt, and pepper. Pour the mixture over the eggplant and toss to combine. Serve immediately with pita bread, or cover with plastic wrap and refrigerate for up to 2 days.

RECIPE NOTE

The eggplant can be roasted in the oven instead of on the stovetop (you won't get the incredible smoky flavor, though). Preheat the oven to 500°F/260°C/gas 10. Prick the eggplant a few times with a fork, and then place it on a rimmed baking sheet. Roast until it is blackened and deflated, about 20 minutes. Remove from the oven and set it aside until it's cool enough to handle, then proceed with the recipe.

Serves 8

2 eggplants (about 1 lb/455 g each)

1 red onion, halved and finely chopped

1 tomato, cored, halved, and finely chopped

1 jalapeño, finely chopped (seeded and ribbed for less heat)

2 tbsp extra-virgin olive oil

2 cups/480 ml plain yogurt

½ cup/20 g fresh cilantro leaves, finely chopped

Juice of ½ lemon

¼ tsp Aleppo pepper

⅛ tsp sumac

1 tsp kosher salt

½ tsp freshly ground black pepper

4 pita breads, warmed in the oven or over a burner and sliced into quarters, for serving

SIMPLE MARINATED PEPPERS

Makes 12 roasted peppers

12 red bell peppers

¼ cup/60 ml extra-virgin olive oil

3 tbsp balsamic vinegar

Kosher salt

6 roasted garlic cloves or 3 fresh garlic cloves

This is an easy but versatile preparation for roasted peppers. I love roasted pepper strips on a freshly toasted baguette with chèvre, or puréed with cream for a simple pasta sauce. I've been making roasted peppers for ages, but when my upstate neighbor Lisa Padgett showed me her straightforward and tasty method (learned from friends in Spain), I changed my ways. Seasoned with balsamic vinegar and roasted garlic, the marinated peppers can even be a side dish to scrambled eggs, quiche, pork chops, or just about anything, really. Roasted garlic makes all the difference, but fresh garlic (use half as much) works, too.

❋ ❋ ❋

Adjust an oven rack to the upper-middle position and heat the broiler to high. Place the bell peppers on an aluminum foil–lined rimmed baking sheet, and broil them until they're blackened on all sides, 12 to 16 minutes. Wrap each pepper in a damp paper towel, and place them in a large paper bag to steam. Set aside for 20 minutes.

Open the bag and remove the peppers. Remove the stems, and turn each pepper upside down over the sink to drain. Peel the blackened skins. Make a lengthwise slit in the peppers so that thy can lay flat, and use a knife to scrape away the seeds.

Whisk together the olive oil, vinegar, and a sprinkle of salt in a 9-by-13-inch/23-by-33-cm baking dish. Place the peppers flat in the baking dish and place the garlic cloves between them. Cover the dish with plastic wrap and refrigerate overnight or up to 1 week before serving.

VARIATION: MARINATED EGGPLANT AND PEPPERS

Reduce the quantity of roasted red peppers from 12 to 8. Slice a 1-lb/455-g eggplant lengthwise into ¼-in-/6-mm-thick slices. Sprinkle both sides with kosher salt, and set aside for 15 minutes. Pat dry, brush with a little olive oil, and place the eggplant on an aluminum foil–lined rimmed baking sheet. Heat the broiler to high and char the eggplant on both sides, 3 to 4 minutes per side. Slice the eggplant into thin strips, and layer with the peppers in the marinade.

RECIPE NOTE: QUICK "ROASTED" GARLIC

For quick roasted garlic, adjust an oven rack so it is in the uppermost position (about 3 in/7.5 cm from the broiler element) and heat the broiler to high. Place the unpeeled cloves on a rimmed baking sheet. Broil the garlic until the paper is brown-black, 2 to 3 minutes. Use tongs to turn the cloves. Repeat until both sides of the garlic are browned, 4 to 6 minutes. Remove the baking sheet from the oven and set the garlic aside to cool. Peel off the skin and store covered in olive oil until ready to use.

SUMMER TOMATO PIE

Serves 6

FOR THE BISCUIT CRUST

2 cups/255 g all-purpose flour

¼ tsp Herbes de Hebron (page 215) or herbes de Provence

1 tbsp baking powder

1 tsp kosher salt

6 tbsp/85 g unsalted butter, cut into small pieces

¾ cup/180 ml milk

FOR THE PIE

2 lb/910 g Roma tomatoes or two 25.5-oz/715-g cans or jars of plum tomatoes, drained and pressed between sheets of paper towels papers to remove excess moisture

⅔ cup/165 g mayonnaise, store-bought or homemade (page 217)

1 tsp Herbes de Hebron (page 215) or herbes de Provence

2 tsp extra-virgin olive oil

2 tbsp roughly chopped fresh basil

1 tbsp finely chopped fresh chives

Kosher salt

Freshly ground black pepper

2 cups/220 g grated aged cheddar cheese

1 tbsp unsalted butter, melted

This tomato pie and I go back more than a decade to Salisbury, Connecticut, and a lovely tea café called Chaiwalla (named for the tea vendors in India) owned and tended to by Mary O'Brien. It was at Chaiwalla where I taught my very first cooking class in 1997. During the course of several weekends, Mary and I got to know each other, and I got to know Mary's über-delicious tomato pie.

A thin, biscuit-style crust props up ripe and juicy Roma tomatoes that are cushioned within a base of sharp aged cheddar and a combination of fresh and dried herbs. The tart is deceptive—while it appears fancy and sophisticated, it couldn't be easier to make, being no more difficult than any rustic-style pie. I often add harissa to the mayonnaise base to give the pie a spiciness that works really well with the sweetness of the tomatoes. Mary insists that the pie is best made the night before you plan on serving it and recommends reheating it in a 350°F/180°C/gas 4 oven for thirty minutes. I trust her implicitly.

❊ ❊ ❊

To make the crust: Place the flour, Herbs de Hebron, baking powder, and salt in the bowl of a food processor and pulse to combine. Add the butter and pulse until there aren't any pieces larger than a small pea. Transfer the mixture to a large bowl and pour in the milk, stirring until the mixture is shaggy and no wet spots remain. Knead just a few times to create a ball of cohesive dough. Use a knife to divide the ball into two pieces, one slightly larger than the other.

Place the larger dough ball on a long sheet of plastic wrap or baking paper and cover with another sheet. Roll the dough out into a 12-in/30.5-cm circle that is about ¼ in/6 mm thick, then place the circle on a baking sheet and refrigerate it for 20 minutes. Repeat with the other dough ball, rolling it out to a 12-in/30.5-cm circle (it will be thinner than the first), and then placing it in the refrigerator to chill.

continued . . .

To make the pie: Preheat the oven to 400°F/200°C/gas 6. Bring a large pot of water to a boil and place a large bowl filled with ice water next to the sink. Slice a small X in the bottom of each tomato and then plunge the tomatoes into the boiling water for 30 seconds. Use a slotted spoon to transfer the tomatoes to the ice-water bath, adding more ice as it melts. Remove the tomatoes from the ice-water bath and place them on a paper towel–lined plate to drain, then peel and slice them into ¼- to ½-in-/6- to 12-mm-thick rounds (if using canned plum tomatoes, skip this step). Carefully remove the seeds and set the tomatoes aside. In a small bowl, whisk together the mayonnaise and Herbes de Hebron, and set aside.

Remove the thicker dough circle from the refrigerator and peel off the top layer of plastic wrap, using the bottom sheet to transfer the crust to a 9-in/23-cm pie pan. Trim any overhang to just ½ in/12 mm over the edge of the dish. Brush the dough with the olive oil, and then arrange half of the tomatoes in overlapping layers in the bottom of the crust. Sprinkle with half of the basil and chives, season with salt and pepper, and finish with an even layer of 1 cup/110 g cheese. Layer the remaining tomatoes over the cheese, sprinkle with the remaining basil and chives, season with salt and pepper, cover with the herbed mayonnaise, and finish with the remaining 1 cup/110 g cheese.

Remove the other rolled-out crust from the refrigerator, peel off the top sheet of plastic wrap, invert the dough over the top of the tart, and peel away the remaining sheet of plastic. Fold the overhang under the edge of the bottom crust and crimp the edges to seal. Brush the top of the crust with the melted butter.

Bake the pie until the crust is golden, 25 to 35 minutes. Remove from the oven and let cool, for at least 1 hour, before serving warm, or let cool for longer and serve at room temperature.

FARM ❀ YARN

TRADING COUNTY FAIR FOR COUNTRY FARE

At the end of August, the Washington County Fair opens for a glorious and fun-filled week of cattle and livestock competitions, scarecrow contests, tractor pulls, pig races, and, of course, lots of festival food. While it's all good fun, experiencing this slice of Americana is always a tad bittersweet, making us hungry to bring change to the North Country lifestyle.

In the city, the talk is all about the farmers in the country who grow the beautiful tomatoes and leafy greens and raise the heritage-breed animals sold in urban farmers' markets and gourmet stores. But in the country, the food at the fair reflects a different story—if it's fried or loaded with fat, it seems like it's at the fair. As a result, Charlie and I dream up ways to bring in more locally grown vegetables and cleaner, greener, and more artisanal-style cooking to the realm of the program. We conspire with others who have similar aspirations (and who have leverage with county leaders and USDA-funded 4-H educational and agricultural program heads). Some programs that we introduced to the fair include a farmers' market stand, where fresh, locally grown produce was sold, and fair-wide recycling.

Our friends Brian Gilchrist and his partner, Jim, from Windy River Farm, always take a ribbon at every level for their beef cattle. Besides running the farm, Brian heads Cornell's Cooperative Extension for Washington County, and he integrated recycled servingware to the fair circuit in 2009. (His future aspiration is set on a coleslaw competition, in which the winner's slaw gets featured as the coleslaw of the day.)

It's little steps like these that we hope will culminate in a big impact down the line. Change comes slowly, and we are excited about the prospect of bringing healthier food (for our bodies and the planet) to the fair to complement the always-popular burger and hot dog stands.

PENNE WITH POPPED TOMATOES AND BACON

A bumper crop of cherry tomatoes, a slab of bacon from Jason Huck's Huckleberry Hill Farm in Mount Holly, Vermont, and our good friend and food novelist Kim Sunée, author of Trail of Crumbs, *provided all the inspiration needed to create this decadent, mouth-watering summer pasta dish. One summer, Kim spent nearly a month on our farm while teaching at Battenkill Kitchen, and she and Charlie turned our kitchen into a seasonal country test lab, cooking up a storm every day using beautiful peak-season ingredients gathered from our garden and from local farms and farmstands. While Charlie and I try to keep our cooking as light on animal protein and fat as possible, we are happy to splurge when it makes sense. The addition of thick-cut slab bacon to this dish brings pleasure that is beyond words! This is truly food fit for gods.*

❄ ❄ ❄

Bring a large pot of water to a boil over high heat. Add the 1 tbsp of salt and the pasta and cook following the package instructions until the pasta is al dente. Drain through a colander and set aside.

While the pasta is cooking, heat the olive oil and pepper in a large frying pan over medium heat until the pepper is fragrant, about 30 seconds. Stir in the rosemary, thyme, and basil and then add the bacon, cooking it until it starts to render some fat, about 1 minute. Stir in the onion and cook until it begins to soften, about 2 minutes, stirring occasionally. Stir in the remaining 1 tsp salt and cook until the onion wilts and the bacon takes on a bit of color around the edges, about 5 minutes.

Add the tomatoes, cover the pan, and cook until the tomatoes are starting to shrivel and shrink (but aren't mushy), 3 to 5 minutes. Stir in the pasta and divide among bowls. Serve with lots of freshly grated Parmigiano-Reggiano cheese.

VARIATION: WINTER PENNE WITH BACON AND CREAM

Substitute ½ cup/120 ml crème fraîche, store-bought or homemade (page 214), and ¼ cup/60 ml cream or milk for the tomatoes. Once the crème fraîche and cream comes to a simmer, add the pasta, toss to coat, and turn off the heat. Serve with lots of freshly grated Parmigiano-Reggiano cheese.

Serves 4

1 tbsp kosher salt, plus 1 tsp

One 14.5-oz/410-g box whole-grain, multigrain, or nutrient-enriched penne pasta

1 tbsp extra-virgin olive oil

¾ tsp freshly ground black pepper

2 tsp finely chopped fresh rosemary

2 tsp finely chopped fresh thyme

1 tsp finely chopped fresh basil

½-lb/225-g slab bacon cut into ½-in/12-mm cubes

1 large red onion, quartered and sliced crosswise

1½ lb/680 g cherry tomatoes, halved if large

Freshly grated Parmigiano-Reggiano cheese for serving

FARM ✻ YARN

A PROUD PANTRY

In today's world, where Americans face a pandemic of diabetes and children are at as much risk of diet-related health issues as adults are, it makes sense to pay attention to each and every ingredient that goes into our food. The first place to start is by reading the nutrition labels on boxes and cans of food. Even a pasta recipe can be made healthier by using whole-grain, multigrain, or nutrient-enriched pasta (Barilla Plus is our favorite house brand). When a pasta is made with some or all whole grain, it has a lower glycemic index. And you'll hardly taste the difference.

Also read the nutrition panels on canned and boxed tomatoes—you might be shocked by the over-the-top sodium levels in just one serving of the canned variety. But tomatoes specially packaged in boxes (Pomí and Lucini are my favorite brands) retain their freshness and flavor without added citric acid, sodium, or preservatives.

Another item that we upgraded in our pantry is all-purpose flour, the workhorse go-to flour for many baking recipes. Instead of always reaching for it, I often use other flours either in combination with or instead of all-purpose to boost the nutritive quality of a recipe. It also opens you up to new textures and consistencies—for example, I make the breading for my fried chicken (see page 133) from a mixture of peanut flour, corn flour, and amaranth or rice flour. Used in tandem, they create a beautifully crisp crust that all-purpose flour

could never replicate. Chickpea flour
(besan) is also in our pantry, we use
it instead of white flour in the batter for Bread *Pakoras* (see page 122).
Others that we keep on hand include
potato flour (for lighter-than-air
cakes), whole-wheat pastry flour (for
pizzas, biscuits, and breads), and
rye flour (for Indian flatbreads and
country bread).

When we first moved to the country, our supermarket didn't carry
these items. All it took was a few
pleasant conversations with the store
manager, and the local Price Chopper
began to carry items we suggested.
Remember, take a few seconds to read
nutrition labels on packaged foods.
The impact on your health and well-
being can be huge—and spread the word.

SHRIMP AND SWEET CORN CURRY

My sister, Seema, has a penchant for following my recipes—and also for changing them to suit her tastes and whims, often with excellent results. This recipe is a prime example. Seema took the instructions for corn curry from my first book, Indian Home Cooking, *and substituted coconut milk for the cream. Her idea worked very well, and, in fact, this is now how I make corn curry in the summertime, always using the incredibly sweet Butter and Sugar corn from Sheldon Farm, in Salem, New York.*

I buy huge tiger shrimp (also called tiger prawns) from Allen Brothers in Chicago. They are impressively massive, succulent, and sweet and are a perfect marriage to the rich coconut milk and fresh corn. That said, any size shrimp work, or eliminate them altogether and substitute peas, green beans, or even sliced baby eggplant. We serve this with basmati, jasmine, or sticky sushi rice. Or do what I do and dunk a piece of crusty bread straight into the sauce—heaven!

❁ ❁ ❁

To make the herb paste: Combine the curry leaves, ginger, lemongrass paste (if using), cilantro, jalapeño, and 3 tbsp water in the bowl of a food processor, and purée into a nearly smooth paste. Set aside.

To make the curry: Heat the canola oil, cumin seeds, and mustard seeds in a large pot over medium-high heat. Cook, stirring occasionally, until the cumin browns and becomes fragrant and the mustard seeds pop, 1 to 2 minutes. Add the curry leaves, chiles, turmeric, and asafetida and cook, stirring, for 1 minute. Then stir in the herb paste, reduce the heat to low, and cook until the mixture is very fragrant, 2 to 3 minutes.

Pour in the coconut milk and the cream, stir, increase the heat to high, and bring to a boil. Reduce the heat to medium-low, stir in the salt, and add the corn and shrimp. Simmer until the shrimp curl and are just cooked through, 2 to 4 minutes, stirring occasionally. Stir in the cilantro and serve.

Serves 6

FOR THE HERB PASTE

40 fresh or 60 frozen curry leaves (see page 215)

3-in/7.5-cm piece fresh ginger, peeled and roughly chopped

2 tbsp frozen ground lemongrass paste (optional)

1 bunch fresh cilantro, leafy parts and tender stems ripped off the tough stems

1 jalapeño or serrano chile, stemmed, and seeded for less heat

FOR THE CURRY

3 tbsp canola oil

1½ tsp cumin seeds

1 tsp brown mustard seeds

15 fresh or 22 frozen curry leaves (see page 215), roughly chopped

3 dried red chiles

¼ tsp ground turmeric

⅛ tsp asafetida (see page 214)

Two 13½-oz/405-ml cans coconut milk

½ cup/120 ml heavy cream, half-and-half, or milk

1 tsp kosher salt

4 cups/615 g fresh corn (from 4 to 6 ears) or frozen corn

2 lb/910 g tiger shrimp (16 to 20 shrimp per pound), peeled and deveined

¼ cup/10 g finely chopped fresh cilantro

SALT-ROASTED WHOLE TROUT

Behind our house is a stream called Black Creek, which happens to be quite famous in these parts for its trout. The length of the creek that winds through our property is one of the most active sections, and it's not uncommon in the early summer for fishermen (some we know; some are complete strangers—see Farm Yarn: Drop-Ins Welcome!, page 46) to come knocking on our front door asking for permission to cast a line. Since Charlie and I don't fish at all, we're happy to grant them access—as long as they leave a few trout for us as a thank-you!

In the late spring, the trout are tiny and small. I'll dunk them into batter and fry them whole. More often, though, fishermen covet a bigger catch, so they'll come later in the season to fish larger trout, often several pounds each. I like to cook the bigger fish simply: buried in a baking dish of kosher salt and lots of fresh herbs and lemon slices and then roasted in the oven. It's very ceremonial to bring the baking dish to the table and crack the protective salt layer open to reveal the fish, steamed to perfection and infused with the delicate flavors of herbs straight from our garden.

❈ ❈ ❈

Heat the oven to 350°F/180°C/gas 4. Remove the leaves from the sprigs of one bunch herbs and place in a food processor along with the salt, coriander seeds, and peppercorns. Process until the herbs are pulverized and the mixture is fragrant.

Spread 2½ cups/565 g of the salt mixture over the bottom of a 9-by-13-in/23-by-33-cm baking dish. Lay the fish, side by side, on top of the salt, and then stuff each fish with one bunch herbs. Divide the lemon slices between the two fish, laying them in an overlapping row on top of the herbs. Close the fish and cover them with the remaining salt mixture, making sure that they are completely buried.

Place the baking dish in the oven, and roast for 45 minutes. Remove the dish and set it aside to rest for 30 minutes before cracking open the top of the salt with a knife and gently removing the caked-on layer of salt with a large spoon. Place the fish on a platter and serve on a bed of herbs (if you have extra) and surrounded by lemon wedges.

Serves 4

3 generous bunches mixed fresh herbs (any combination of lemon verbena, lovage, oregano, parsley, rosemary, sage, summer savory, or thyme), plus extra for serving (optional)

6 cups/1.2 kg kosher salt

¼ cup/20 g coriander seeds

2 tbsp whole black peppercorns

2 whole trout (about 1½ lb/680 g each), butterflied and frames removed

3 lemons, 2 thinly sliced, plus 1 cut into wedges for serving

GARAM MASALA ROAST CHICKEN

Serves 4

1 tsp canola or grapeseed oil

3 tbsp Garam Masala (page 216)

1 tbsp kosher salt

One 3½- to 4-lb/1.6- to 1.8-kg chicken

2 tbsp balsamic vinegar

When my coauthor, Raquel, calls with an idea, discovery, or suggestion, I listen. The mother of two young boys and wife of a well-traveled (albeit finicky) film and music distributor, she always has to be on top of her game. There is no place for mediocrity or the ordinary. So when Raquel came up with this version of roasted chicken without any added fat, I knew I was in for a discovery. She rubs garam masala under and on the chicken skin and then splashes the bird with balsamic vinegar for color and crispness. When I'm in the mood to splurge, I like to take duck or goose fat and rub it all over the chicken (see the Variation on the facing page). It gives Raquel's lean chicken a naughty, crispy, decadent taste.

❀ ❀ ❀

Set an oven rack to the lower-middle position and heat the oven to 400°F/200°C/gas 6. Line a rimmed baking sheet with aluminum foil and place a wire roasting rack on the sheet. Grease the roasting rack with the canola oil and set aside. Mix the garam masala with the salt and set aside.

Place the chicken on a cutting board and slide your fingers under the skin of the breast, separating the skin from the meat and making a pocket. Place your fingers where the leg connects to the body and work your fingers down around the thigh and leg, separating the skin from the meat, creating a pocket between the thigh and leg meat and the skin. Place 2 tsp of the garam masala mixture under the skin of each breast and under the skin of each thigh, rubbing it all along the entirety of the meat. Rub the remaining 2 tsp of the garam masala mixture over the skin of the chicken and inside the cavity. Tie the legs together with butcher twine, and tuck the wings behind the back.

Place the chicken, breast-side down, on the roasting rack and roast for 30 minutes. Remove the sheet from the oven, brush the back of the chicken with half of the vinegar, turn the chicken breast-side up, brush with the remaining vinegar, and roast for an additional 30 minutes to 1 hour (depending on the size of the chicken), or until an instant-read thermometer inserted into the thickest part of the thigh reads 165°F/75°C. Remove from the oven, and let rest for 10 minutes before carving and serving.

VARIATION: NOT-SO-LEAN CHICKEN

In a small bowl, mash 6 tbsp/85 g room-temperature unsalted butter with 3 tbsp of the garam masala and salt mixture. Proceed with preparing the chicken for roasting as described, dividing the spiced butter between the breasts and thighs, and massaging the chicken from above the skin to work the spiced butter along the meat. Rub the surface and inside of the cavity with the remaining 1 tbsp spice blend.

Brush 3 tbsp melted duck or goose fat (just warm it in the microwave until it is liquefied) over the surface of the chicken and 1 tbsp inside the cavity. Place the chicken on the prepared roasting rack and roast as instructed. After turning the chicken, dab the surface with another 1 tbsp duck fat and continue roasting as directed. This chicken is especially wonderful roasted over potatoes and onions.

JUICY TURKEY-CHEDDAR BURGERS

Inspiration for this recipe came from my lamb burger recipe, in which I combine ground lamb with lots of spices and a combination of Parmigiano-Reggiano and Pecorino cheeses. Richard Arakelian, a chef colleague, asked me why I never use ground turkey in a burger, and, furthermore, why I rarely use American cheeses, like cheddar, in my recipes. I interpreted his question as a challenge, and this is how my turkey-cheddar burgers came to be.

First, I gently fry herbs and spices, like curry leaves and cumin, with chopped red onions, then I add this mixture, along with shredded cheddar, chopped jalapeños, and fresh cilantro to ground turkey. The result is a turkey burger unlike any you've ever had—absolutely exploding with flavor and masala. The burgers are also delicious made with ground white or dark meat chicken or ground pork.

❋ ❋ ❋

Place 1 tbsp of the canola oil, the curry leaves, cumin seeds, black pepper, and red pepper flakes in a large frying pan over medium-high heat. Cook, stirring often, until the cumin seeds are fragrant and lightly browned, about 2 minutes.

Add the onion and cook, stirring often, until translucent, 2 to 3 minutes. Transfer the mixture to a bowl and set aside to cool.

Place the turkey in a large mixing bowl and gently knead in the cheese, jalapeño, cilantro, and salt. Stir in the onion mixture and form into four patties.

Wipe out the frying pan with a paper towel. Return the pan to medium-high heat for 2 minutes, add the remaining 1 tbsp oil, and then add the patties. Reduce the heat to medium and cook until the patties are browned, about 4 minutes. Flip, and cook the other side until browned and the center is cooked to your preferred doneness (I like mine slightly pink). Place the burgers on the toasted buns, dollop with raita and chutney, and serve.

continued . . .

Serves 4

2 tbsp canola oil

8 fresh or 12 frozen curry leaves, finely chopped (see page 215)

1 tsp cumin seeds

½ tsp freshly ground black pepper

¼ tsp red pepper flakes

½ small red onion, finely minced

1¼ lb/570 g ground turkey (preferably dark meat or a combination of white and dark meats)

¾ cup/85 g tightly packed shredded cheddar cheese

½ jalapeño, finely diced (seeded and deveined for less heat)

¼ cup/10 g chopped fresh cilantro leaves

1 tsp kosher salt

4 burger buns, toasted

Raita (page 218) for serving

Tomato-Onion-Peanut Chutney (page 221) for serving

VARIATION: PARTY MEATBALLS

Preheat the oven to 375°F/190°C/gas 5. Instead of dividing the meat mixture into four patties, divide it into golf ball–size portions. Coat your hands with a little olive oil, and then gently roll the portioned meat between your hands until round, then slightly flatten into disc-shaped patties. Place the patties on a wire rack set over a rimmed baking sheet and brown the meatballs until they're cooked through. Skewer on toothpicks or mini bamboo skewers and serve with Raita or Tomato-Onion-Peanut Chutney on the side.

STRAWBERRIES-AND-CREAM ICE CREAM

Half-and-half from Battenkill Valley Creamery (see page 108), eggs from our chickens, and strawberries from our favorite strawberry farmer, Brian Talmadge of Black Lab Farm, combine to produce the richest, goldest, and creamiest strawberries-and-cream ice cream you can imagine. I always start out with a crème anglaise base and never tire of the fact that while my anglaise in the city is tinted pale yellow, in the country it almost looks like melted butter due to the quality of the cream and the vibrancy of our egg yolks. Of course, the stars of the show are small, intensely sweet strawberries that we get by the flat. They're the same summer berries we use in our superb garnet-colored strawberry jam (see page 109). You'll only use 1 cup/240 ml strawberry syrup in the ice cream. Save the remaining 1½ cups/360 ml syrup, for drizzling over pancakes or biscuits, in the refrigerator for 3 days, or freeze it for up to 3 months for the next time you're craving strawberry ice cream.

❀ ❀ ❀

To make the syrup: Slice 1½ lb/680 g of the strawberries in half and quarter the remaining ½ lb/230 g. Place the halved strawberries in a medium saucepan along with the sugar, lemon zest, and lemon juice. Bring to a simmer over medium-high heat, then reduce the heat to medium-low and simmer gently, stirring occasionally, until the strawberries break down and become jammy, about 10 minutes. Stir in the quartered strawberries and cook until they are very soft and nearly melted into the sauce, about another 10 minutes. Pour the sauce into a medium bowl, let cool to room temperature, and then chill in the refrigerator for several hours before using.

To make the ice cream base: Pour the half-and-half into a medium heavy-bottomed saucepan and bring to a simmer. Turn off the heat. If you're using vanilla bean paste or extract, skip to the next step. If you're using a vanilla bean, slice the bean in half lengthwise. Using the tip of a knife,

continued . . .

Makes about 1¼ qt/1.2 L

FOR THE STRAWBERRY SYRUP

2 lb/910 g strawberries, hulled

½ cup/100 g sugar

Zest of 1 lemon

1½ tbsp fresh lemon juice

FOR THE ICE CREAM BASE

3 cups/720 ml half-and-half

1 vanilla bean, or 1 tsp vanilla bean paste or vanilla extract

6 egg yolks

¾ cup/150 g sugar

scrape the seeds into the half-and-half, add the bean halves, and whisk. Cover the saucepan, and set it aside for 30 minutes.

In a large bowl, whisk the egg yolks with the sugar until thoroughly combined. If you've used a vanilla bean, strain the vanilla-infused half-and-half through a fine-mesh sieve and into the eggs, whisking constantly. If you're using vanilla bean paste or extract, simply whisk the eggs with the sugar and half-and-half, and proceed with the next step (you'll add the vanilla later).

Set a medium bowl into an ice-water bath and place it next to your stove. Return the egg mixture to the saucepan and place it over medium-high heat. Cook, stirring slowly and continuously with a wooden spoon, until you can draw a clear line through the custard on the back of the spoon, about 5 minutes. (Don't allow the custard to boil; this could cause the eggs to curdle.)

Strain the base through a medium-mesh sieve and into the chilled bowl in the ice-water bath. If using vanilla bean paste or extract, whisk it in now. Whisk for 30 seconds to cool slightly, then cover the custard flush with plastic wrap and refrigerate until it's cold, at least 1 hour or preferably longer (the base will last for up to 3 days in the refrigerator).

Transfer the custard to an ice-cream maker and freeze it according to the manufacturer's instructions until it reaches a soft serve–like consistency. With the machine running, pour in 1 cup/240 ml of strawberry syrup and let it churn in until it is completely incorporated. Transfer the ice cream to a container, cover, and freeze until the ice cream is firm, at least 4 hours or up to 3 days. Let the ice cream stand at room temperature for 5 to 10 minutes before scooping and serving.

FARM ✿ YARN

BATTENKILL VALLEY CREAMERY

Opening a jug of half-and-half or cream from the Battenkill Valley Creamery is like unwrapping a gift. There is always a layer of thick cream on top—I just can't help sighing at the sight of it.

Seth McEachron, a fifth-generation dairyman, has dedicated his life to rethinking how his family runs its dairy business and makes milk. Many other farmers in the area give their milk to large dairies, but Seth decided that his family would continue to be a single-origin operation, selling milk like they did decades ago:

in clear glass bottles (the milk actually goes from cow to bottle within eight hours!).

We go out of our way to pick up our whole milk and superthick chocolate milk directly from the dairy. We love seeing the Holsteins, Jerseys, and Holstein-Jersey crossbreeds that generously give us their milk. At the shop, there is a cash box on the counter and milk in the reach-in cooler—customers abide by the honor system, leave their payment, and walk out happy.

SEASONAL JAM

Every summer, Charlie and I have a ritual: We make jam, and lots of it. We buy many flats of fruit from local farmers (or if we have a particularly lucky season, we gather the fruit from our own trees and shrubs) and slowly cook giant batches of preserves, marmalades, chutneys, and jams. Rather than using pectin as a preservative and thickener, I prefer to cook the jam slowly for several hours over low heat until it thickens naturally and gels. More of a spoon fruit than a supermarket spreadable, our jarred jams are given as gifts for holidays, housewarmings, and thank-yous. You'll need a very large pot to make large batches of jam. For a smaller batch, simply halve (or quarter) the following recipe. If using blueberries, blackberries, or raspberries, crush half of the berries (a potato masher works perfectly) and add the remaining berries whole. This creates a nice texture.

❉ ❉ ❉

Makes 18 pt/8.5 L

Seasonal fresh fruit, hulled and halved if large and pitted if necessary (apricots, blackberries, blueberries, cherries, gooseberries, nectarines, peaches, raspberries, sour cherries, strawberries, etc.; refer to the chart on page 112 for ingredient amounts)

Sugar (refer to the chart on page 112)

Lemon zest and juice (refer to the chart on page 112)

¼ tsp salt

Additional seasonings (refer to the chart on page 112)

Place a ceramic plate in the freezer (you'll use the chilled plate to test the gel of the jam). Stir together the fruit, sugar, lemon zest and juice, salt, and any additional seasonings in a large 15-qt/14.2-L stockpot. Bring the mixture to a boil over medium-high heat, stirring often. Reduce the heat to medium-low and gently cook the jam until a spoonful mounds nicely when dabbed onto the chilled plate, doesn't run excessively when you tip the plate, and leaves a semithick trail when you run your finger through the middle of the dollop, anywhere from 1 hour to 2½ hours, depending on the fruit (see the chart on page 112).

continued . . .

While the jam cooks, prepare your jars, lids, and bands. Bring a large pot of water to a boil. Add the jars (you will probably have to sterilize the jars in batches depending on the size of your pot—or you can run them through your dishwasher and keep them warm until filling) and sterilize for 10 minutes. Use rubberized jam tongs to transfer the jars, open-end down, to a clean kitchen towel until you're ready to fill the jars with hot jam (you don't want the jars to cool completely; make sure they're still slightly warm when you fill them). Place the bands and lids in a separate pot of simmering water (don't boil the lids because that could affect their ability to seal properly). Once you're ready to fill the jars, remove the bands and lids from the water and drain on the kitchen towel.

Use a funnel to fill the jars with jam to within ¼ in/6 mm of the jar's lip. Securely screw on the lids and bands, and then place the jars back into a large pot of boiling water for 10 minutes (make sure the water completely covers the jars) to process (you will probably have to do this in a few batches). Use tongs to transfer the hot jars from the water to the kitchen towel and let them sit out at room temperature for 24 hours before testing the seal on the jars and storing the jam. (To test the seal, just press the top of the lid—it should be taut without any give). If the jar lid bounced back, then it didn't seal properly. Boil the jar for 10 minutes more, and let sit out for 24 hours before retesting.

Use jam within 1 year.

SEASONAL JAM CHART

I often add unexpected ingredients to my jams and preserves, giving them a beauty and flavor that many find a welcome change from your average plain strawberry, blueberry, or peach preserves. This chart lists some of my favorite stir-ins to add to the master recipe on page 109:

	Fruit	Sugar	Lemon	Other Flavors
Apricot Jam (Cooks for 1 hour and 10 minutes)	20 lb/9 kg	8 lb/3.6 kg	4 lemons, zested and juiced	½ cup/70 g whole apricot kernels, 3 tbsp ground ginger
Blueberry Jam (Cooks for 2 hours)	20 lb/9 kg	8 lb/3.6 kg	6 lemons, zested and juiced	3 tbsp ground ginger
Peach Preserves (Since peaches have ample natural pectin, the jam only needs to cook for about 1 hour and 10 minutes total)	16 lb/7.2 kg	8 lb/3.6 kg	4 lemons, zested and juiced	½ cup/70 g whole apricot kernels, 3 tbsp ground ginger, ½ tsp finely ground black pepper, ½ tsp crushed saffron, ¼ tsp cayenne pepper
Raspberry and Blood Orange Jam (Cooks for 2 hours)	12 lb/5.4 kg raspberries; 8 lb/3.6 kg blood oranges, zested and juiced	14 lb/ 6.4 kg		
Sour Cherry Jam (Cooks for 2 hours and 30 minutes; makes 14 pt/6.6 L)	20 lb/9 kg	8 lb/3.6 kg	Zest of 2 lemons	
Strawberry Jam (Cooks for 2 hours and 15 minutes to 3 hours)	20 lb/9 kg	10 lb/ 4.5 kg	4 lemons, zested and juiced	¼ cup/60 ml vanilla bean paste, or 2 to 3 vanilla beans (depending on how plump they are); ½ tsp freshly ground black pepper
Sweet Cherry Jam (Cooks for 2 hours)	20 lb/9 kg	10 lb/ 4.5 kg	4 lemons, zested and juiced	⅓ cup/75 ml kirsch liqueur (add once the jam is removed from heat)

FARM ❉ YARN

U-PICK, U-SHARE

Meg and Rob Southerland are the own-ers of Gardenworks, a berry farm in Washington County. In an effort to encourage locals to pick berries and to boost what they have to sell in the store, they offer this incredible incentive: Pick as much as you can in the fields, and you'll leave with half of the bounty at no charge. The remaining half stays at Gardenworks to get sold at the farmstand. It's a brilliant plan where everyone wins—especially the people who get to eat the berries!

CHAPTER THREE

FALL

Embracing Autumnal
Transitions and Traditions

Fall is fleeting here in the North Country. We only have until mid-October before the cold reality of the coming winter settles in for its six-month hold on the region. Short as it may be, these six weeks are positively blissful, filled with piercing blue skies, blazing foliage, and air scented with smoke from wood-burning fireplaces.

Charlie and I strive to stretch each day to its maximum. I pluck the last tomatoes of the season from our garden, while Charlie and visiting friends plant fall bulbs (the gigantic earthworms get my skin crawling—they're many times fatter than India's scrawny variety!), and we make an extra effort to never miss the weekend farmers' market. Though summer is our peak houseguest season, we still get many visitors, all hungry for autumn's colors that only this part of the country can share. Nestled between Vermont's Green Mountains and the Adirondacks to our west, we are lucky enough to get the best shows from both ranges.

While we have plenty of Pippin apple trees on our property, we go apple picking elsewhere if only for an excuse to go on an indulgent leisurely drive through the countryside. Charlie even eases up on the gas so we can coast through especially stunning Rembrandt-like passes brushed with leaves of gold, amber, and burnished orange.

I'd be lying if I didn't admit that we deceive ourselves into pretending that fall will continue forever. The truth, however, is that the cold and bitter winter is just around the bend. So, between pressing cider and making pints of apple butter, we're also ensuring that every chicken, goat, human, and struc-ture on our property is braced for winter.

We receive our final hay deliveries now, and they fill the farm with the sweet smell of dried grass and legumes. Making sure that our animals are comfort-able becomes a top priority. Charlie inspects the goat barns for cracks that need to be sealed to keep the barn as warm as possible, while I tend to my hens and roosters, giving a keen eye to spots where we might need a heat lamp to keep the birds cozy throughout the cold months. We make sure our pond bubbler is in working order, for, unlike some who let nature take over and allow ponds to freeze, we like to keep our ducks and geese happy with a liquid (albeit cold) pool to swim in.

Fall is the season of trimming—trees, branches, hooves, and coats. Leaves are raked into towering piles for composting. One of my favorite fall activities is shearing the sheep and Angora goats (shearing is one farm chore we always leave for the more experienced!). We deliver the thick and supremely soft fiber to a local mill for processing into roving and yarn. One of my goals is to learn how to spin my own wool, but for now we have it spun for us. Once I receive the thick twists, I can begin to imagine the sweaters and scarves that I'll knit from it.

To the amusement of many, whenever I'm in town on a Tuesday evening, I stop by the local "stitch and bitch" club down the road. Knitting and gossiping with the ladies of Washington County is one of my favorite cold-weather pastimes.

While I'm practicing my purling, Charlie is preserving. North Country is blessed with many artisanal cheesemakers, and the last production of chèvre, that tangy fresh white pâté cheese, is made now. Charlie submerges crottins in Italian extra-virgin olive oil with fresh herbs, like verbena and rosemary, clipped from our garden. He adds a few peppercorns and red chiles and sets the cheese aside to cure. What a quick and amazing treat it is to offer guests a real taste of summer farmhouse life preserved to savor throughout the fall and winter. An olive oil– brushed and charred baguette is all you need for a heavenly snack or first course with a sip of something crisp and special from our wine cabinet.

We delay the final gathering of the herbs from our garden for as long as we can because, to us, this act truly signals winter to steamroll over our pathway of slate steps leading to the house. Charlie snips dozens of sprigs before the first frost gets them, bundles the bunches with twine, and hangs them upside down from coat pegs to dry in the mudroom. In the months to come, they offer a touch of country whimsy and an intoxicating fragrance. Nothing beats crumbling these home-dried herbs into batches of marinara for lasagna, a rub for a roast, chutney, frittatas, and soup. Our guests are always impressed to learn that these chic, charming bouquets came from our own little garden.

In our kitchen, we continue to think locally as we cling somewhat desperately to the last of our garden's offerings. Corn and squash continue to entertain us with their flourish, as well as strong and resolute broccoli, hardy herbs, and Brussels sprouts. Other than these brave few, the garden begins to wither away, reminding us about life's inevitable movement from one season to the next. Our guest roster slows, and our calendar shows fewer visits from faraway friends. It's nothing to feel down about, though, as late fall brings local friends back to our table, the friends who were occupied all summer long with their harvests and animals. Farmers and neighbors are eager to congregate around our dining table and hungry to eat, gossip about the season past, and share dreams of the spring to come.

Just as we're ready to accept our cold-weather fate, we get a final burst of Indian summer that gives us a temporary reprieve from the dipping mercury. Gardenworks, the local berry farm, gets a blast of late-season raspberries and blueberries, so even procrastinators like me get a chance to preserve. Even as the leaves fall and grass browns, the hills become invigorated by shocks of orange, this time from the thousands of pumpkins that sprout up throughout the area. Before we know it, fall's first frost blankets the farm and nestles us into a cold, quiet stillness.

CHAI CIDER

When Charlie and I discovered that we had a plot of Pippin apple trees on our property, we were so excited that we couldn't wait for the fall harvest. Untended for nearly a decade, the trees were wild and gnarly like something out of a children's fairy tale. Lucky for us, their homely appearance didn't affect the crisp, incredibly floral tasting, palm-size apples that sprang from the trees in September.

  We like to keep the cider in a saucepan on the stove on the lowest heat possible (or in the carafe of a drip coffeemaker on the warm setting). The result is a warm spiced-apple perfume that smells one hundred times better than any potpourri or scented candle. Cider is the absolute essence of the countryside in the fall.

❀ ❀ ❀

Combine the cider, brown sugar, ginger, apples, and kumquats in a slow cooker.

Wrap the quartered oranges, cinnamon sticks, cloves, and peppercorns in a large piece of cheesecloth and tie to prevent from opening. Add to the pot, and cook on the lowest possible heat until the apples are completely tender and soft, 2½ to 3 hours.

Once you are ready to serve, steep the tea bags in the hot cider for 10 minutes. Remove and discard along with the spice packet.

Ladle the cider into mugs with a shot of cognac (if using). Top each cup with some of the apples, kumquats, and cranberries, and serve.

continued . . .

Makes about 4 qts/3.8 L; serves 8 to 10

4 qts/3.8 L apple cider or apple juice

½ cup/100 g packed brown sugar

¼ tsp ground ginger

3 apples (preferably Pippins or Granny Smiths), thinly sliced and cut crosswise into bite-size pieces

1 cup/110 g halved kumquats or 2 small seedless oranges, sliced into eighths

3 oranges, quartered and seeded

3 cinnamon sticks

2 tsp whole cloves

1 tsp freshly ground black peppercorns

3 Darjeeling tea bags

Cognac or Armagnac (optional)

Fresh cranberries (optional)

VARIATION: STOVETOP CIDER

If you don't have a slow cooker, follow the recipe using a large pot over low heat and reduce the cooking time to 45 minutes to 1 hour.

VARIATION: APPLE CIDER GLAZE

A great use for any leftover cider, this glaze makes a delicious finishing addition to pork chops or a ham.

Strain the leftover apple cider to remove any solid bits of fruit or spice. Measure the strained cider, then pour it into a saucepan and bring to a simmer over medium-high heat. While the cider warms, dissolve ½ tsp cornstarch with 1 tbsp cider in a small cup or bowl for every 1 cup/ 240 ml cider in the saucepan. Add the cornstarch slurry to the simmering cider and stir until it thickens. Remove from the heat and brush the glaze over a ham or pork chops, or store in an airtight container for up to 1 week. Reheat gently (don't let it come to a simmer) before glazing.

HARVEST APPLE-CRAISIN CHUTNEY

While apples are definitely a hallmark of upstate New York's autumn harvest, they were also a delicious part of my growing up in India. "An apple a day" was a rule that my mother and my maternal grandmother followed religiously—at least while apples were in season. Every morning at the breakfast table, my grandmother, Nani, would begin the ritual of peeling and slicing an apple. She'd hand out the slices one at a time, to my brother, my sister, and then myself, followed by whoever else might be joining us that morning. She'd continue this way, passing out apple slices like a Vegas card dealer, until each family member had eaten the equivalent of one crisp, juicy apple.

❋ ❋ ❋

Heat the canola oil with the chiles, fennel seeds, and cumin seeds in a large saucepan or frying pan over medium-high heat until the cumin is browned, 2 to 2½ minutes. Stir in the paprika and cook for 15 seconds, then add the apples and salt and cook until the apples get juicy, 3 to 4 minutes. Stir in the sugar, vinegar, and craisins, then reduce the heat to medium and cook, stirring often, until the apples are soft, sticky, and deeply golden and caramelized, 35 to 45 minutes. Taste for seasoning, transfer to a plastic container, and refrigerate for up to 1 week, or ladle into dry and sterilized jars and can according to the manufacturer's instructions.

VARIATION: SAVORY-SPICY APPLE-CRAISIN CHUTNEY
To add a savory and spicier taste to the chutney, add 1 tbsp ground coriander, ½ tsp cayenne pepper, and ¼ tsp asafetida (see page 214) to the oil along with the other spices.

Makes about 2 cups/475 ml

3 tbsp canola oil

3 to 6 dried red chiles

1½ tsp fennel seeds

1 tsp cumin seeds

½ tsp sweet paprika

3½ lb/1.6 kg tart, crisp apples (like Rhode Island Greening or Granny Smith), peeled, cored, quartered, and thinly sliced crosswise

1½ tsp kosher salt

¼ cup/50 g sugar

2 tbsp white wine vinegar

½ cup/75 g craisins

BREAD PAKORAS

Makes 12 pakoras

4 cups/960 ml canola or vegetable oil, plus more if needed

1½ cups/140 g chickpea flour (besan)

½ tsp baking soda

1 large red onion, very finely chopped

1 jalapeño, very finely chopped (seeded and deribbed for less heat)

1 cup/40 g fresh cilantro leaves, very finely chopped

1 tbsp *chaat* masala (see page 214)

¾ tsp ajwain seeds (carom seeds)

½ tsp Garam Masala (page 216)

¼ tsp cayenne pepper

¼ tsp ground turmeric

½ tsp freshly ground black pepper

2 tsp kosher salt

6 slices white, whole-wheat, or multigrain sandwich bread, halved diagonally

Tamarind Chutney (page 219) or ketchup for serving

Bread pakoras *are a wonderful breakfast treat. Growing up in India, I was lured from bed on many mornings by the scent of them frying in our kitchen. Essentially a slice of bread dipped in a spiced chickpea batter and fried, these are one of my favorite breakfast treats to make for visitors.*

❊ ❊ ❊

Heat the canola oil in a deep frying pan or medium saucepan (if using a saucepan you'll only be able to fry one *pakora* at a time) over high heat to between 350°F/180°C and 375°F/190°C on a digital thermometer. You should have about 2 in/5 cm of oil in the pan; add more as needed.

While the oil heats, whisk together the chickpea flour, baking soda, onion, jalapeño, cilantro, spices, and salt in a large bowl. While whisking, gradually pour in 1¼ cups/300 ml lukewarm water until you have a thick batter.

Dip a bread triangle into the batter, making sure it is nicely coated on both sides, and carefully slide it into the hot oil. If you're using a deep frying pan, repeat with another bread slice (take care not to overcrowd the pan, otherwise the *pakoras* will stick together). The bread should float to the top immediately and be surrounded by lots of tiny bubbles. Drizzle 1 tsp batter over the top of the bread and baste the top with hot oil to set the batter. Fry until golden brown, about 5 minutes, and then carefully flip the bread slice over and fry the other side until golden brown. Using a kitchen spider or slotted spoon, remove the *pakora* from the oil and set aside on a paper towel–lined plate to drain. (You can keep the fried *pakoras* warm on a baking sheet in a 250°F/120°C/gas ½ oven while you wait for the remaining *pakoras* to fry.) Dip and fry the remaining bread slices, and serve warm with chutney on the side.

RECIPE NOTE: DOUBLE-DECKER BREAD PAKORAS

This is my absolute favorite way to use leftover mashed potatoes. First, season the potatoes with a pinch of cayenne, some *chaat* masala, lime juice, chopped jalapeño, and chopped cilantro. Spread a few spoonfuls between two slices of bread and press firmly to seal. Dip the sandwich in the *pakora* batter, and then fry it. Wow, what an amazing snack.

FARM ❀ YARN

THE WEED WE GREW TO LOVE

When we moved into the farmhouse, I knew right away that I wanted to have an herb garden, even though I had never gardened before in my life. Charlie and I set out and bought an assortment of lovely herbs, from summer savory to lavender to several varieties of basil, mint, oregano, and thyme. We planted everything along a slate stone path that leads up to the side entrance of the house, and it was a cook's dream—for awhile. Then we were invaded by weeds, especially one particularly invasive weed that Charlie, no matter what he tried, couldn't get rid of. It grew and grew and couldn't be eliminated, so Charlie did some research. His findings were shocking—this weed, the one we cursed and pulled from the ground in handfuls, was also known as bishop's weed, or Ethiopian cumin, which was another term for *ajwain*, small striped seeds commonly used in Indian cooking!

Our bishop's weed wasn't exactly the same as the *ajwain* variety used in Indian foods, but like Thai basil is to globe basil, it was similar enough, and we were excited about our discovery all the same. In Indian cooking, *ajwain* is often used in veggie stir-fries and combined with chickpea flour to give batter a bitter, thymelike flavor. Discovering this herb was just another sign that we were meant to live in this turmeric-colored farmhouse.

FRENCH ONION SOUP

Serves 6

2 tbsp unsalted butter

1 tbsp olive oil

½ tsp freshly ground black pepper, plus more if needed

½ tsp Herbes de Hebron (page 215) or herbes de Provence

Red pepper flakes

3 medium red onions, halved and thinly sliced

2 large shallots, halved and thinly sliced

1 tbsp kosher salt, plus more if needed

3 garlic cloves, finely minced

¼ cup/60 ml port

¼ cup/60 ml red wine (preferably a Merlot or Merlot blend)

6½ cups/1.5 L warm vegetable broth, plus more if needed

2 cups/480 ml water

1 small Parmigiano-Reggiano rind (optional)

1 baguette

Extra-virgin olive oil

1 cup/100 g grated Gruyère cheese

My vegetarian French onion soup is unapologetically deep and robust thanks to onions and shallots that are caramelized until intensely browned and frizzled. Red wine, port, and vegetable broth bring layers of sophistication to this simple soup, though, as with many recipes, the end result can only be as good as its individual parts. Our Parmigiano-Reggiano is the real deal, garlic is often from a local grower, and the olive oil is good quality. No onion soup is complete without the requisite Gruyère-laden toasts dunked into each bowl just before serving. Be sure to make a few extra cheese toasts for each serving—in my mind, they're the key ingredient to great French onion soup!

❀ ❀ ❀

Heat the butter with the olive oil in a large Dutch oven or soup pot over medium heat. Once the butter is melted, add the pepper, Herbes de Hebron and anywhere from a pinch to ¼ tsp red pepper flakes, cooking the spices until fragrant, stirring occasionally, 1 to 2 minutes. Stir in the onions, shallots, and salt and, once the onions are just starting to brown around the edges, after 3 to 5 minutes, add the garlic. Reduce the heat to medium-low and cook, stirring every few minutes, until the mixture is deeply browned and crispy, about 40 minutes. (If the mixture begins to get too dark and the browned bits are not scraping off the bottom of the pot, splash the pan with a bit of vegetable broth to loosen the browned bits, using a wooden spoon to scrape them up and into the mixture. Don't turn your back on this mixture—it can go from caramelized to burned in a short time—like risotto, it needs your attention.)

Pour in the port and red wine, and stir and scrape the bottom of the pan to release the browned bits. Simmer until the liquid is absorbed by the onions but the pan is still wet, about 30 seconds. Add the warm vegetable broth, water, and Parmigiano-Reggiano rind (if using) and bring to a boil. Reduce the heat to medium-low and gently simmer for 30 minutes. Taste for seasoning, adding more salt and pepper if necessary.

While the soup cooks, adjust an oven rack to the upper-middle position and heat the broiler to high. Slice the baguette on the bias into ¼-in-/ 6-mm-thick slices. (If you are serving the soup in wide-mouthed bowls, make the slices longer by angling your knife more. If your bowls are smaller, adjust the length of the bread slices accordingly.) Place the slices on an aluminum foil–lined baking sheet and drizzle a little extra-virgin olive oil over the top. Broil until browned and toasted, about 1 minute. Remove from the oven, turn the slices over, and sprinkle the tops of the untoasted bread with the cheese. Broil until the cheese is browned and bubbly, 1 to 2 minutes.

Divide the hot soup into bowls. Place a few slices of Gruyère toast, cheese-side up, in each bowl and serve immediately.

PEANUT CHAAT

Serves 8

2 tbsp peanut oil

12 fresh or 18 frozen curry leaves (see page 215), very finely chopped

¼ tsp cumin seeds

6 cups/875 g roasted, salted peanuts

1 large red onion, very finely chopped

1 jalapeño, halved and seeded (leave the seeds for a spicier flavor)

1 large tomato, halved, seeded, and finely chopped

½ cup/20 g fresh cilantro leaves, finely chopped

1½ tsp *chaat* masala (see page 214)

¼ tsp cayenne pepper

½ tsp kosher salt

Juice of 1 lime, or more to taste

This snack is one of my favorite chaats to make, as it never fails to surprise and delight with its contrast of crunchy peanuts, crisp curry leaves, tender onions, and juicy tomatoes (chaat means "to lick" in Hindi). It is so simple and basic but so satisfying and delicious, plus peanuts are a wonderful cholesterol-free source of protein, which is especially important if you eat a primarily meat-free diet.

Peanut Chaat was a big hit when I made it for the annual Chef's Brunch during the Al Fresco Weekend at the Courthouse Community Center in Salem, New York. I went through 60 lb/27 kg of peanuts in the blink of an eye, and had I been feeling more generous, I'm sure I could have dished out 100 lb/45 kg of peanut chaat without a problem. You can make it as mild or as spicy as you like by adding to or subtracting from the cayenne and chaat masala called for here.

❊ ❊ ❊

Heat the peanut oil, curry leaves, and cumin seeds in a large frying pan over medium-high heat, stirring occasionally, until the curry leaves are crisp and the cumin seeds are golden, about 2 minutes. Add the peanuts and cook, stirring often, until they're golden and glossy, 4 to 5 minutes. Stir in the onion and jalapeño, and cook just until the onion begins to soften, about 2 minutes.

Turn off the heat; stir in the tomato, cilantro, *chaat* masala, cayenne, and salt; and then stir in the lime juice. Using tongs or a spoon, mix well and serve warm.

VARIATION: SOUTH INDIAN PEANUT CHAAT

For a southern Indian flavor, omit the *chaat* masala and add ½ tsp brown mustard seeds along with the curry leaves and cumin seeds. Add 2 tsp Sambhaar Powder (page 219) along with the cilantro and remaining ingredients.

CHAAT FRIES

These homemade fries are absolutely worth the time and effort it takes to make them. Panditji, my parents' cook, always made them for my brother and me on days when we had cricket practice. He knew we'd invade the house with our teammates, all of us ravenous. We'd keep devouring these fries, which are flavored with a spice blend called chaat masala that is at once salty and savory and wonderful, until he ran through as many potatoes as he could possibly have in the house—often up to 20 lb/9 kg!

Chaat masala is integral to chaat and is perhaps my favorite Indian seasoning. Sprinkle it on just about anything, from grilled corn to roasted sweet potatoes.

Serves 4 to 6

3 lb/1.4 kg Yukon gold potatoes

2 tsp chaat masala (see page 214)

¼ tsp cayenne pepper

1½ tsp kosher salt

1 tsp freshly ground black pepper

6 cups/1.4 L canola or vegetable oil

❋ ❋ ❋

Peel the potatoes and slice them lengthwise into ⅓-in-/8-mm-thick planks. Slice each plank into ⅓-in-/8-mm-wide sticks. As you're slicing the potatoes, place them in a large bowl of ice water so that they don't oxidize and discolor. Mix together the chaat masala, cayenne, salt, and pepper in a small bowl and set aside.

While you peel the potatoes, slowly heat the canola oil to 275°F/135°C in a wok or saucepan (you should have at least 2 in/5 cm of oil in the pan). Place a clean kitchen towel on your worksurface and lift about one-third of the potatoes out of the bowl, shaking off as much of the excess water as possible. Place them on the kitchen towel to drain, blotting the potatoes dry as best as you can (an extra towel and paper towels may come in handy).

Heat the oven to 250°F/120°C/gas ½. Drop the first batch of potatoes into the hot oil, reduce the heat to medium, and, using a frying spider or slotted spoon, turn the potatoes often so that they cook evenly. Once the temperature of the oil dips to 250°F/120°C, after 5 to 7 minutes, increase the heat to medium-high and cook the potatoes until they become golden brown, about 7 minutes more. Transfer the fries to a paper towel–lined plate to drain and then place on a rimmed baking sheet. Sprinkle with one-third of the spice mixture and keep them warm in the oven while you cook the remaining potatoes in batches. Serve immediately.

"I CAN'T BELIEVE IT'S NOT MEAT" RAGU OVER FETTUCCINE

Serves 8

1 large red onion

4 medium carrots

4 medium celery stalks

1 lb/455 g cremini mushroom caps

¼ cup/60 ml extra-virgin olive oil

3 whole cloves

1-in/2.5-cm cinnamon stick

¼ tsp freshly ground black pepper

⅛ tsp dried basil

⅛ tsp dried oregano

⅛ tsp dried rosemary

⅛ tsp dried thyme

2 tsp salt, plus 1 tbsp

4 cups/900 g canned or boxed crushed tomatoes

½ cup/120 ml dry red wine (like Grenache)

1 tsp Herbes de Hebron (page 215) or herbes de Provence

2 tbsp unsalted butter

2 lb/455 g whole-grain, multigrain, or nutrient-enriched fettuccine pasta

Freshly grated Parmigiano-Reggiano cheese for serving

This is the ragu I turn to when I crave something robustly flavored, hearty, and substantial. It is so deeply seasoned that many dinner guests never guess it is a vegetarian sauce. The trick is to chop the vegetables in a food processor, so they give the sauce heft and body and the slightly rough texture of a meat sauce. For a spicier version, add ½ tsp red pepper flakes and double the amount of black pepper. Sometimes I like to add a dash or two of balsamic vinegar at the end for a slightly sweeter sauce.

❋ ❋ ❋

In the bowl of a food processor, process the onion until it's very fine but not a paste. Scrape it out into a small bowl and set aside. Process the carrots and celery until fine and scrape into another bowl. Process the mushrooms until fine and set aside (they can stay in the food processor bowl).

Heat the olive oil with the cloves, cinnamon stick, pepper, basil, oregano, rosemary, and thyme in a large pot over medium-high heat until the cinnamon stick begins to unfurl, about 2 minutes.

Add the onion and the 2 tsp salt and cook, stirring often, until the onion is starting to brown, about 5 minutes. Stir in the carrots and celery and cook, stirring occasionally, until the mixture is browned, about 12 minutes. Stir in the mushrooms and cook until they release their liquid, stirring occasionally, about 4 minutes. Add the tomatoes and cook, stirring occasionally, until the liquid is somewhat reduced, about 4 minutes.

Pour in 1 cup/240 ml water and the wine and bring to a boil. Reduce the heat to medium-low and simmer, stirring occasionally, for 30 minutes or up to 2 hours for a more deeply flavored ragu (if after 1 hour the soup looks thick and jammy, add an extra ½ cup/120 ml water). Add the Herbes de Hebron and butter and cook, stirring occasionally, for 5 minutes longer to allow the flavors to come together.

While the ragu simmers, cook the fettuccine. Bring a large pot of water to a boil. Add the remaining 1 tbsp salt and the fettuccine and cook, following the package instructions until the pasta is al dente. Drain the fettuccine in a colander and turn it out into the ragu. Toss to coat the pasta with the sauce and divide among 8 bowls. Top with Parmigiano-Regggiano and serve.

FARRO AND MUSHROOM BURGERS

The farm has become a wonderful draw for friends from around the world who want to come to visit us and experience our new life. I encourage everyone to make our home their home, with full kitchen privileges. Charlie and I were smitten when our friend Joyce Goldstein, the incredibly talented award-winning chef, trendsetter (she steered the café kitchen at Chez Panisse for years), and author of more than twenty-seven cookbooks, came to visit us at the farm. We happily cooked together and learned from each other.

While I shared my ideas and techniques for cooking with Indian flavors, Joyce introduced us to farro and how wonderfully delicious it is. Farro is now always in my pantry. I love using it in this recipe for veggie burgers. In addition to protein and heart-healthy fiber, the texture it contributes is incredibly hearty. You can sandwich the burgers in a bun (top with Tomato-Onion-Peanut Chutney, page 221) or eat it as a cutlet with chutney and a green salad on the side. When Charlie, Raquel, and I were working on recipes for this book, Raquel came to the farm eight-months pregnant; she and her four-year-old son devoured these burgers with such voracity that I am convinced neither missed the presence of meat! If you can't find farro, you can make the burgers with quinoa instead.

❋ ❋ ❋

Makes 10 patties

¾ cup/125 g farro

1 lb/455 g red potatoes (about 3)

1 sprig fresh rosemary

1 sprig fresh thyme

6 tbsp/85 g unsalted butter

1 tsp freshly ground black pepper

1 lb/455 g cremini mushroom caps, finely chopped

1¼ tsp kosher salt

5 to 8 tbsp/75 to 120 ml extra-virgin olive oil

3 shallots, finely chopped

1 tbsp dry white wine, dry vermouth, or water

½ cup/50 g finely grated Parmigiano-Reggiano cheese

1 cup/50 g panko bread crumbs

Bring 2¼ cups/540 ml water to a boil in a medium saucepan. Add the farro, return to a boil, cover, and reduce the heat to medium-low, cooking until the farro is tender, about 30 minutes. Turn off the heat, fluff the farro with a fork, cover, and set aside.

While the farro cooks, boil the potatoes. Bring a large saucepan of water to a boil, add the potatoes, return the water to a boil, and cook until a paring knife easily slips into the center of the largest potato, about 20 minutes. Drain and set aside. Once the potatoes are cool, peel them and place them in a large bowl.

continued . . .

Remove the needles and leaves from the rosemary and thyme sprigs and place them in a large frying pan along with the butter and pepper. Cook over medium-high heat, stirring occasionally. Once the herbs start cracking, after about 1½ minutes, add the mushrooms and salt. Cook until the mushrooms release their liquid and the pan is dry again, 6 to 7 minutes, stirring often. Transfer the mushrooms to the bowl with the potatoes and set aside.

Heat 1 tbsp of the olive oil in the same frying pan over medium-high heat. Add the shallots and cook until they are soft and just starting to brown, about 2 minutes. Add the wine and stir to work in any browned bits from the bottom of the pan. Turn off the heat and scrape the shallots into the bowl with the mushrooms and potatoes. Add the Parmigiano-Reggiano along with the cooked farro. Use a potato masher or fork to mash the ingredients together.

Form the mixture into ten patties. Place the panko in a shallow dish and press the top and bottom of each patty into the panko to evenly coat. Heat 4 tbsp/60 ml of the olive oil in a clean large frying pan over medium-high heat. Add five patties and cook on each side until nicely browned and crusty, 8 to 10 minutes total. Remove the patties from the frying pan and place them on a plate. Repeat with the remaining patties, adding more oil between batches if necessary. Serve hot.

PEANUT FRIED CHICKEN

The fried chicken that I serve at my restaurant, Dévi, has a true follow-ing. The secret is in the spice-packed buttermilk brine and the spiced flour mixture I use for the breading. I apply those same tactics to this completely gluten-free recipe for fried chicken. Instead of wheat flour, I use a combi-nation of peanut flour (see Farmhouse Resources, page 222), cornmeal (for crunch), and either amaranth or rice flour (for a shatteringly crisp coating). Fried in a cast-iron frying pan, every bite of this spice-laden country staple instantly transports me from my quiet farm to the bazaars and souqs of faraway lands where the air is laced with spices and the staccato of marketplace banter.

❁ ❁ ❁

To make the brine: Whisk together the buttermilk, salt, sugar, garam masala, coriander, pepper, paprika, and cayenne in a large bowl until the salt is dissolved.

Add the chicken and turn to coat in the brine. Cover with plastic wrap and refrigerate overnight or up to 36 hours. (To save space in the fridge, divide the chicken between two 1-gl/3.8-L resealable plastic bags, mak-ing sure to evenly cover with brine.)

Pour the peanut oil into a large pot or deep cast-iron frying pan, making sure the oil fills the pan to a depth of 1 to 1½ in/2.5 to 4 cm. Heat the oil over medium heat until it reaches 350°F/180°C on an instant-read ther-mometer. Remove the chicken from the brine and place on a plate. Whisk both flours and the cornmeal with the spices in a large bowl. Add the chicken to the dry mixture and toss around to coat evenly. Let the chicken sit in the spiced flour while the oil heats. Add the chicken to the hot oil and fry until golden brown on all sides, about 12 minutes for the wings and legs, and 15 minutes for the breasts and thighs. (If at any time during frying the temperature of the oil dips below 300°F/150°C, increase the heat to medium-high.) Using tongs, transfer the fried chicken to a cooling rack set over a rimmed baking sheet and let cool for at least 5 minutes before sprinkling with salt and serving. Serve warm (the chicken can be kept warm in a 200°F/95°C oven if you like) or at room temperature.

Serves 4

FOR THE BRINE

3 cups/720 ml buttermilk

¼ cup/50 g kosher salt

2 tbsp sugar

2 tsp Garam Masala (page 216)

1 tbsp ground coriander

1 tsp freshly ground black pepper

½ tsp sweet paprika

¼ tsp cayenne pepper

One 3½- to 4-lb/1.6- to 1.8-kg chicken, cut into 8 pieces and breasts halved crosswise if large

4 to 6 cups/960 ml to 1.4 L peanut oil for frying

1½ cups/135 g peanut flour

½ cup/80 g amaranth or rice flour

1 cup/160 g cornmeal

1 tbsp Garam Masala (page 216)

2 tsp freshly ground black pepper

2 tsp ground turmeric

1½ tsp sweet paprika

½ tsp ground cinnamon

Kosher salt for serving

FARM ✿ YARN

THE BATTENKILL KITCHEN

Charlie and I strive to help make our community a food-centric one. One cause we are particularly committed to is the Battenkill Kitchen, a shared-use licensed facility that is available for food start-up ventures, as well as culinary education classes.

Say you have a bumper blueberry crop one year—well, for just $25 an hour, you can rent the kitchen to make blueberry pies or to can blueberry jam to sell. The kitchen is licensed, certified, and maintained, so entrepreneurs don't have to worry about the red tape of production. In addition, the kitchen is equipped for large-scale production, so people can make large batches of whatever it is that they plan to sell.

Charlie has been a Battenkill Kitchen board member since 2008 and has focused on raising funds to keep the kitchen sparkling, maintained, and equipped. To raise money, he brings in top chefs, like Joyce Goldstein, Hiroko Shimbo, and Rose Levy Beranbaum, to teach culinary classes to intimate groups of twelve to sixteen students. In addition to the students who pay the full face value for a spot in the class, the kitchen offers a free spot to a Salem Food Pantry customer so that he or she can learn how to

incorporate the fresh vegetables received from the pantry into interesting dishes to make at home for his or her family. Other classes emphasize in-season fruits and vegetables and are taught by Annette Nielsen, a local foodie, journalist, and community activist.

As much produce as possible is brought in from the food pantry so that chefs can highlight various ways to cook with veggies grown on nearby farms. In addition, many farms donate produce in exchange for a reduced class fee—Hicks Orchard gives the kitchen the crispest and most flavorful heirloom New York state apples, while Slack Hollow Farm donates greens and alliums; corn and potatoes are regulars from Pat Sheldon's farmstand, and Meg Southerland of Gardenworks gives beautiful local berries. While North Country may not have the most sophisticated restaurant scene, we are trying our hardest to bring the best culinary experiences and quality produce to the people who live here.

HERBED PHEASANT BREASTS WITH SPICED POMEGRANATE REDUCTION

Serves 6

FOR THE STOCK

Reserved pheasant wings and bones

2 large carrots, peeled and thickly sliced

2 celery ribs, thickly sliced

1 large yellow onion, thickly sliced

3 qt/2.8 L water

2 cups/480 ml dry red wine

6 sprigs fresh thyme

2 bay leaves

2 tbsp finely chopped fresh flat-leaf parsley

2 whole black cardamom pods

1 cinnamon stick

1 tsp whole black peppercorns

1 tsp kosher salt

Rafi Taherian, the head of Yale Dining, invited me to New Haven, Connecticut, to show the staff how to add some masala to their meals for students, faculty, and employees, and since then, I have been back to visit often. On one occasion, I dined in the Presidents' Room and was served a beautiful feast prepared by chef David Kuzma. As soon as I tasted his sublime pheasant and the beautiful squash and cranberry gratin served alongside it, I knew they were dishes that I had to re-create at the farm.

Eating pheasant is not an everyday experience. You either need to be connected to local farmers, hunters, and purveyors or very well endowed with the resources to order anything from anywhere. Well, I most definitely belong to the former club. All I need to do is reach out to the many people in my community who raise pheasants for meat, and they're often happy to share a few birds.

This dish is at once refined and rustic, as only pheasant can be. The meat is intensely aromatic from a quartet of fresh herbs and pungent garlic and gets a sweetness from maple syrup and a touch of balsamic vinegar. Instead of a traditional meat gravy, I use pomegranate molasses to conjure a rich sauce that is spiced with cinnamon and cardamom. The aroma of pheasant in my kitchen always grounds me in this season of hunting; game; and big, bold flavors.

Ask a butcher to debone and fillet the breasts (but don't leave the shop without the removed bones, so you can make the sauce; ask the butcher for the caul fat, too). Be sure to ask that the wing joint be left on so that it can be frenched like a lamb chop. It makes an absolutely exquisite presentation. And if you cannot find pheasant, rest assured, this is delicious made instead with boneless chicken thighs.

❊ ❊ ❊

Make the pheasant stock: Heat the oven to 450°F/230°C/gas 8. Place the reserved pheasant bones on a rimmed baking sheet or in a roasting pan and roast them until golden brown, 30 to 40 minutes. Transfer the bones to a large stockpot. Add the carrots, celery, onion, 2½ qt/2.5 L of the water, the red wine, thyme, bay leaves, parsley, cardamom, cinnamon, peppercorns, and salt. Bring the mixture to a boil, skim the foam off the top, and reduce the heat to medium. Bring the remaining 2 cups/

480 ml water to a boil in a small saucepan and use it to deglaze the roasting pan. Pour the water and browned bits from the pan into the stockpot. Simmer the pheasant broth for 3 to 4 hours (4 hours for a more concentrated stock). Turn off the heat and let cool slightly before straining the broth into a clean pot. Discard the bones and vegetables and refrigerate the broth until you're ready to make the sauce.

Heat the olive oil with the basil, rosemary, thyme, parsley, garlic, and ½ tsp of the pepper in a medium frying pan over medium heat until the garlic is fragrant, 2 to 3 minutes. Immediately scrape the mixture into a bowl large enough to hold the pheasant, and stir in the maple syrup, vinegar, and salt. Set aside to cool, then add the pheasant breasts, turn to coat in the mixture, cover with plastic wrap, and refrigerate overnight.

Heat the oven to 450°F/230°C/gas 8. If using caul fat, rinse it in a large bowl in several changes of cold water until the water runs clean. Lay the caul fat (or bacon) flat on a cutting board (if using bacon, overlap the strips slightly). Remove a pheasant breast from the marinade and place it, skin-side down, onto the fat and wrap the fat around it to completely enclose the breast. If there is extra caul fat, trim it away. Place the wrapped breasts, seam-side down, in a roasting pan and cook until the exterior begins to crisp and an instant-read thermometer inserted into the thickest part reads 150°F/65°C, 18 to 20 minutes. Remove the pan from the oven and loosely tent the pheasants with a sheet of aluminum foil until its internal temperature reaches 165°F/75°C, 15 to 20 minutes.

While the pheasant rests, bring half of the pheasant stock to a simmer over medium-high heat (freeze the remaining stock for another time). Decrease the heat to medium and simmer until it is reduced to about 2 cups/480 ml. Reduce the heat to medium-low and stir in the molasses. Whisk in the butter until it is just melted, taste, and season with salt if necessary. Place the breasts on a cutting board and carve them into thin slices. Turn off the heat and serve the sauce alongside the carved pheasant breasts.

½ cup/120 ml extra-virgin olive oil

2 tbsp finely chopped fresh basil

2 tbsp finely chopped fresh rosemary

2 tbsp finely chopped fresh thyme

2 tsp finely chopped fresh flat-leaf parsley

2 garlic cloves, very finely chopped

2 tsp finely ground black pepper

3 tbsp maple syrup (preferably grade B dark amber)

1 tbsp balsamic vinegar

1 tsp kosher salt

10 frenched pheasant breasts, or 5 whole pheasants (breasts boned and filleted, wing tips removed, and wing joints frenched)

10 oz/280 g caul fat or 10 strips thin-cut bacon

½ cup/120 ml pomegranate molasses

2 tbsp unsalted butter

Kosher salt for finishing

BRAISED KID SHANKS
AND LENTILS

Serves 6 to 8

⅓ cup/80 ml extra-virgin olive oil

Eight 12-oz/340-g goat shanks

2 sprigs fresh rosemary

1 tbsp kosher salt

2 tsp freshly ground black pepper

3 bay leaves

2 dried red chiles

2-in/5-cm cinnamon stick

6 garlic cloves, smashed with the flat side of a chef's knife

4 medium red onions, halved and thinly sliced

2 shallots, halved and thinly sliced

1 tsp Herbes de Hebron (page 215) or herbes de Provence

One 750-ml bottle dry red wine

1½ lb/680 g black beluga lentils

6 cups/1.4 L water, plus more if needed

Having grown up in India, I've never found it a stretch for me to cook goat meat. But cooking kid meat (that from young goats) that comes from our own herd, well, that was not easy, especially at first. I've had to make peace with eating an animal that I watched grow and frolic, that I fed and cared for. With help from Angela Miller, my good friend, neighbor, and literary agent, I rationalized that, because we provide for the goats and raise them humanely and with love, we should feel okay with completing their circle of life. Selling goat meat helps sustain the farm and the other animals that are a part of our farm's family. So with the exception of the few boys that we use as studs, we are now at peace with knowing that the other boys born every spring will be raised for meat. We thank them for coming into the world and for providing us with nourishment.

Unlike mutton and the meat from older goats, kid meat has a neutral taste and takes on other flavors beautifully. This recipe is not too far off from dalcha *meat stews eaten by Indian Muslims. The key is to brown the shanks on all sides for a deep and rich-tasting sear. I like using small black beluga lentils, though French green lentils or* sabut masoor *(reddish-brown whole Indian lentils) also work nicely. Indians cook lentils until they are very soft and almost saucy (like a dal), and that is how the lentils in this dish are prepared, making it lovely served alongside fluffy rice, creamy mashed potatoes, or couscous.*

❀ ❀ ❀

Heat the oven to 250°F/120°C/gas ½.

Heat the olive oil in a large Dutch oven or other heavy ovenproof pot over medium-high heat for 2 minutes. Add the shanks, rosemary, salt, and pepper and brown the shanks on all sides, 15 to 20 minutes total (depending on the size of the shanks and your pan, you may need to brown them in two batches). Use tongs to transfer the shanks from the pot to a large plate and set aside.

continued . . .

Add the bay leaves, chiles, and cinnamon stick to the pot and cook until the chiles begin to brown, about 1 minute. Reduce heat to low, add the garlic, and cook, stirring often, until it becomes crispy, 2 to 3 minutes. Increase the heat to medium-high; stir in the onions, shallots, and Herbes de Hebron; and cook, stirring often, until the onions are dark brown and crisp, 15 to 20 minutes. If the onions begin to stick or become too dark, splash them with a bit of water and stir and scrape them up from the bottom of the pan to keep them from burning.

Once the onions are deeply caramelized and browned, pour in the wine and cook until the onions are plump and jammy again, about 5 minutes. Stir in the lentils and cook until they begin to stick to the pan, 2 to 3 minutes. Add the shanks back to the pan and stir them around. Pour in the water. If the shanks aren't covered, add more water until they are just submerged. Bring the water to a boil and then turn off the heat. Cover, place the pot in the oven, and cook until the meat easily pulls off the bone, about 2½ hours.

Remove the pot from the oven and place it on the stovetop. Using tongs, transfer the shanks to a serving platter and loosely cover with a sheet of aluminum foil to rest. Bring the lentils in the pot to a simmer until the remaining liquid in the pot is reduced, 3 to 5 minutes (or longer if you prefer a thicker sauce). Serve the lentils over the shanks.

FARM ❖ YARN

LOVE IS IN THE AIR

Come to our farm in the fall, and you might find yourself wondering what that musky smell is around the goat barn. Well, it's called rut, and it occurs when the fall mating season arrives; the bucks do just about everything that is too embarrassing to see, let alone write about in a cookbook! The girls and the bucks dance in ways you can't even begin to imagine, and the adorable, downy results are born in the spring.

Timing is really everything—if the goats mate too early, then come late February and early March, poor Charlie will find himself in the barn in the middle of the night hugging a just-born and still-slick kid close to his chest, using his body heat to warm the newborn. If all goes according to plan, though, and mating begins in the late fall, the kids are born in late March and early April, when it isn't so cold for the babies (or for Charlie). I don't think that there is a better welcome than rolling up our gravel driveway and being greeted by the sight of baby goats chasing each other in circles on the front lawn. I just have to remind our fall visitors that enduring the strong perfume in the air is worth it!

SPICY PULLED PORK

Serves 6 to 8

FOR THE SPICE PASTE

1 tsp cumin seeds

1 tsp coriander seeds

10 dried red chiles

½-in/12-mm cinnamon stick

8 whole cloves

6 whole green cardamom pods

10 whole black peppercorns

½ tsp ground turmeric

6 garlic cloves, minced

2-in/5-cm piece fresh ginger, peeled and minced

2 tbsp white vinegar

Juice of ½ lemon

½ tsp kosher salt

2 lb/910 g boneless pork butt or shoulder, well trimmed

2 very ripe medium tomatoes, quartered, or one 14.5-oz/400-g can whole peeled tomatoes, drained

2 medium red onions, quartered

3 tbsp canola or grapeseed oil

1 tsp salt, plus more if needed

6 to 8 hearty Kaiser rolls or brioche buns

Coleslaw for serving

Pickles for serving

Just south of our farm is Michael Yezzi and Jennifer Small's Flying Pigs Farm in the Battenkill River Valley. They raise rare heritage-breed pigs, like Large Blacks, Gloucestershire Old Spots, and Tamworths, which yield incredibly moist and flavorful meat. The pigs are raised in a loving environment on grains, vegetables, and fruits. This pulled-pork recipe really benefits from full-flavored, well-marbled pork like theirs (pork butt is my first choice, but it can be hard to find; a picnic shoulder is a fine alternative). Pulled pork is a natural with cornbread, in quesadillas with pico de gallo and guacamole, rolled into a soft-shell taco with spicy chutney, or even layered with basmati rice to make a pseudo layered biryani casserole.

❊ ❊ ❊

To make the spice paste: Combine the cumin seeds, coriander seeds, chiles, cinnamon, cloves, cardamom, and peppercorns in a spice grinder and grind to a coarse powder. Transfer to a 1-gl/3.8-L resealable plastic bag and add the turmeric, garlic, ginger, vinegar, lemon juice, and salt. Mash the outside of the bag to mix the ingredients. Add the pork to the paste, mix to coat, and marinate for at least 2 hours or overnight.

Meanwhile, purée the tomatoes and onions in a food processor, and set aside.

Heat the canola oil in a large heavy-bottomed pot over medium-high heat. Add the pork and the marinade and cook, stirring often, for 10 minutes. Stir in the tomato-onion purée and the salt and bring to a boil. Add enough water to cover the meat, return to a boil, reduce the heat to a simmer, and cook, covered, until the meat is tender and shreds easily, about 2 hours for pork shoulder and about 3 hours for pork butt. Let the pork cool in the pan and then shred, taste for salt, and divide onto the buns. Top with coleslaw and serve with pickles on the side.

SHIRRED EGGS WITH
PULLED PORK

Gently baked in the oven until the eggs are just set, this makes for a wonderfully elegant breakfast or brunch, especially considering it's made from leftovers, or rather, "planned overs." I'll often set aside the pork that I'll need to make this dish and freeze it in a resealable plastic bag for use on a cold, brisk morning. We serve it in ramekins straight from the oven with toast, cornbread, or Grandma Mae's Biscuits.

❋ ❋ ❋

Heat the oven to 450°F/230°C/gas 8. Grease six 6-oz/180-ml ramekins or shallow individual-size gratin dishes with the butter. Place ⅓ cup/ 90 g shredded pork in each ramekin and make a deep well in the center. Crack 1 egg into each well and sprinkle with the salt and cumin.

Place the ramekins on a rimmed baking sheet in the oven and bake until the whites are cooked and the yolk is barely set, 10 to 14 minutes (or longer if you like your yolks cooked through). Serve with hot sauce and biscuits on the side.

Serves 6

2 tbsp unsalted butter, at room temperature

2 cups/565 g shredded Spicy Pulled Pork (facing page)

6 large eggs

1 tsp kosher salt

½ tsp Toasted Cumin (page 221) or cayenne pepper

Hot sauce for serving

Warm Grandma Mae's Biscuits (page 77), 12 buttered toast slices, or warm cornbread for serving

RABBIT STEW WITH
PORCINI AND PICHOLINES

*In the country, people find themselves cooking with all types of proteins
other than chicken, pork, and beef, and it's not without a laugh that I
found myself cooking rabbit at the farm. Anyone who knows me would
probably never believe that I absolutely love this Southern France–inspired
rabbit stew and happily make it for guests, as it has become a favorite
in our kitchen. I have David Setford, the executive director of The Hyde
Collection in Glens Falls, to thank for introducing me to this wonderfully
hearty collection of autumnal ingredients, including robust rabbit, earthy
dried porcini, and mild picholine olives. It is sublime over fusilli or rotini
pasta. You can remove the pits from the olives if you like, but picholines
are rather small and cumbersome to pit. We keep it rustic and serve the
olives whole—just forewarn your dinner guests that the olives have pits.
I like to serve this hearty stew on plates with roasted potatoes or fresh
crusty bread.*

❁ ❁ ❁

Preheat the oven to 300°F/150°C/gas 2. Whisk together the flour, 1 tsp
of the pepper, and ½ tsp of the salt in a large bowl. Pat the rabbit dry with
paper towels and then dredge it through the seasoned flour. Place it on a
large plate and set aside.

In a large heavy-bottomed pot over medium-high heat, heat the olive oil
with the bay leaves and remaining 1 tsp pepper until it begins to smoke,
about 4 minutes. Add the rabbit and brown it on both sides, about
10 minutes total (it won't be cooked through). Transfer the rabbit to a
large plate and set aside.

Add the thyme, onions, and remaining 1 tsp salt to the pot and cook,
stirring often, until the onions start to soften, about 2 minutes. Stir in the
garlic and cook, stirring occasionally, until it's fragrant, about 1 minute,
and then stir in the olives, mushrooms, and wine. Bring the mixture to
a boil and then return the rabbit to the pot, wedging the rabbit into the
broth and covering it with the onions, olives, and broth. Return the mixture to a simmer, reduce the heat to low, cover, and braise until a fork
can easily pull the meat from the bone, about 2 hours. Taste for salt and
adjust if necessary, divide among plates, and serve.

Serves 6

½ cup/60 g all-purpose flour

2 tsp freshly ground mixed
peppercorns or black pepper

1½ tsp kosher salt, plus more
if needed

One 2½-lb/1.2-kg rabbit, cut into
6 pieces (2 drumettes, 2 thighs,
2 breasts); heart, liver, and kidneys
saved for making Country Rabbit
Terrine with Pistachios and Pernod
(page 181) or Rustic Rabbit Pâté
with Juniper Berries (page 183)

¼ cup/60 ml extra-virgin olive oil

4 bay leaves

2 tbsp finely chopped fresh thyme
(preferably lemon thyme)

1 lb/455 g cipollini onions, peeled

8 garlic cloves, smashed

1 lb/455 g unpitted picholine olives

1 oz/30 g dried porcini mushrooms

One 750-ml bottle Pinot Blanc wine

FARM ❋ YARN

LOCK, STOCK, AND TWO SMOKING BARRELS

Charlie and I both romanced the country life long before we moved here. It was an Anne Willan cookbook, *From My Château Kitchen*, that gave us a taste for a slower-paced, food-centric life. Through her eloquent prose and decadent recipes, we pretended that we, too, lived on a beautiful country estate instead of in a financial district high-rise. After a few years of dreaming, we turned our wishes into a reality and bought our beautiful farm in Washington County.

All our friends thought we were mad when we told them we were buying an honest-to-goodness farm four hours north of New York City, but we knew that this was the right choice for us, even if it did mean weeding in Ralph Lauren. For the first few weeks, family and friends helped us move in and transition the farm into our new home. Then life returned to business as usual—I packed up and left to tend to the restaurant in the city and then to travel to a conference. Charlie was alone in our new home. Which was wonderful . . . until he had to run out on an errand. He went to lock the door and realized that the house had no locks! Not even one! Now, we're all for being free in the country, but locking the door, well, that was a comfort we weren't ready to let go of.

Everything happens more slowly on country time, and so it took weeks to get the locks installed. During that time, poor Charlie was petrified of leaving the house open. After days upon days of being housebound, he finally had to let go of his fear and just leave. When he returned home, he had to check every room, closet, and corner before he deemed it safe to sink into a chair and relax.

We found ourselves in a slightly different situation when it came to the safety of our livestock. When we invested in nearly 150 goats, sheep, alpacas, geese, ducks, chickens, and guinea fowl, we were naive in our understanding of one of the most basic facts about having animals in the country: protecting them from predators.

From the beginning, even before our beautiful four-legged kids grazed the property, we found that the question most people asked was whether we owned a gun. In West Virginia, where Charlie grew up, they practically hand you a rifle along with a rattle—hunting is a part of the lifestyle. In India, however, guns are highly controlled. I maintained that educated and civilized people living in the twenty-first century did not need guns, even if they were living in the countryside. So we did not and, would not, own a gun, end of story.

Well, it's amazing how quickly perspectives change when a roving pack of hungry coyotes decides to set up camp on your land! While playing tour guide in NYC to Charlie's grandma, we received a phone call from a long-standing hobby-farmer friend whom we had put in charge of our farm until we returned. She said that one of the kid goats had died. She was in a panic. The experience was so traumatic for her that she left our farm and animals in the charge of someone else for the remainder of the agreed-upon time and stored the dead goat in the corncrib—where we keep our animal feed!

We quickly returned home and began to sort through the ordeal, starting with cleaning out the corn-crib (we scrubbed it from top to bottom to ensure that no animals would get sick, just in case the goat had died from a disease) and ending with a site inspection of the farm, which is when Charlie noticed that the electric fence that controls the perimeter was flashing big zeros. He walked the fence line and discovered that an apple tree had split and fell right smack on it. I didn't connect the non-working fence with the death of the goat until a few days later, when shopkeepers, neighbors, and delivery people reported coyotes in our field. Charlie raced out to the barn and, wouldn't you know it, our alpacas, which protect livestock much like sheepdogs, weren't hanging out close to the barn where they usually are but were instead guarding the periphery

of the pasture. Once we saw them charging real live coyotes, we deduced that a pack must have gotten into the field when the fence was down. When we repaired the fence, we had inadvertently trapped them in our pasture. We couldn't be sure that a coyote had killed the goat, but, nonetheless, we made it our mission to get the coyotes off our land before there was another incident.

We bought a rifle. Within a few days, Charlie picked off the coyotes (I did shoot the rifle a few times, but my aim was horrible), and we're happy to report that we haven't had a predator on the farm, or a need to use our rifle, since.

AUTUMN PEAR AND
CRANBERRY COBBLER

*This cobbler's breathtaking fuchsia color is only a preamble to its deva-
statingly delicious flavor bolstered by two unusual additions: a pinch of
cayenne pepper and ground black peppercorns. These spices provide a
little back heat that counters the sweet and tangy cobbler filling beautifully—if you didn't know there was cayenne in the cobbler, you'd never
guess it.*

*The beauty of cobbler is that just about any fruit you could imagine
tastes delicious in the filling. Feel free to substitute apples, apricots, nectarines, peaches, or plums for the pears, or use all berries. Fresh early-
summer sour cherries are a delightful substitute for the cranberries, as
are any kind of berry from wild strawberries to gooseberries and even
spring rhubarb.*

❋ ❋ ❋

Preheat the oven to 375°F/190°C/gas 5.

To prepare the fruit: Combine the pears, berries, and cranberries in
a large bowl and toss together with the sugar, cornstarch, lemon zest,
lemon juice, spices, and salt. Transfer the fruit to a large pot and cook
over medium-high heat until the fruit breaks down into a jamlike consistency, about 5 minutes, stirring once or twice. Spread the fruit into a
9-by-11-in/23-by-27-cm baking dish, and set aside.

To make the topping: Whisk together the egg and milk and set aside.
Place the flour, 2 tbsp of the sugar, the baking powder, and salt in a food
processor and pulse to combine. Add the butter and pulse until the
butter is worked in and there are no bits larger than a small pea. Add
the liquid to the dry ingredients while pulsing until all of the liquid is
added and just a couple of dry patches remain. Transfer the dough to
a large bowl and work by hand once or twice just to combine.

Break the dough into 12 small chunks and arrange them over the fruit.
Sprinkle the biscuits with the remaining 2 tbsp sugar. Bake the cobbler
until the biscuits are golden brown, 25 to 30 minutes. Remove from the
oven and let cool for at least 30 minutes. Serve with heavy cream, whipped
cream, or vanilla ice cream.

Serves 8

FOR THE FRUIT

5 ripe Bartlett or Anjou pears,
peeled, cored, and cut into thin
wedges

2 cups/300 g fresh berries
(like blackberries, blueberries,
raspberries, or strawberries)

1 cup/110 g fresh cranberries

1 cup/200 g sugar

1 tsp cornstarch

Zest of 1 lemon,
plus juice of ½ lemon

½ tsp ground ginger

¼ tsp ground black peppercorns

⅛ tsp cayenne pepper

Pinch of freshly grated nutmeg

Pinch of salt

FOR THE TOPPING

1 large egg

3 tbsp whole milk or heavy cream

1 cup/115 g all-purpose flour

4 tbsp/50 g sugar

1½ tsp baking powder

½ tsp salt

6 tbsp/85 g frozen butter, cut into
small pieces

Heavy cream, whipped cream, or
vanilla ice cream for serving

APPLE UPSIDE-DOWN CAKE

Serves 8

14 tbsp/200 g unsalted butter

1½ cups/300 g dark brown sugar

½ cup/120 ml tangerine, orange, or blood orange juice, preferably freshly squeezed

½ cup/120 ml cognac

3 firm-fleshed apples like Granny Smith (our favorite is Belle de Boskoop), peeled, halved, cored, and chopped into 1-in/2.5-cm cubes

1½ cups/190 g whole-wheat pastry flour or cake wheat flour, sifted

½ cup/100 g granulated sugar

2 tsp baking powder

¼ tsp salt

1 large egg, at room temperature

½ cup/120 ml milk, at room temperature

1 tsp vanilla bean paste or vanilla extract

When I was a young boy in India, my grandmother, Nani, was famous for her pineapple upside-down cake. She'd somehow whip it up effortlessly just before serving dinner, bake it while we ate, and then serve it, still hot from the oven, after our plates vanished from the table. Charlie and I continue this wonderful tradition of fresh-from-the-oven desserts when we entertain. Delicious sweet treats need not be complicated or filled with drama, and that is why this recipe is one of our favorites. Charlie often puts it together (he is the baker in our family) as the last thing that happens in the kitchen before dinner is served, and then we bring it out to the dinner table, still in the cast-iron frying pan, and flip it out to a chorus of oohs and aahs. It's a great dessert to make while others watch, not just to show off how easy it is to make, but also to give them the confidence to re-create it in their homes. If you don't have a cast-iron frying pan, buy one! It is a sound and inexpensive investment—I also use one to make Grandma Mae's Biscuits on page 77. If you remain stubborn, then make the caramel in a medium saucepan, pour it into a 9-in/23-cm cake pan, add the apples, and proceed with the recipe as instructed below.

❁ ❁ ❁

Heat the oven to 400°F/200°C/gas 6.

Melt 6 tbsp/85 g of the butter in an 8-in/20-cm cast-iron frying pan over medium heat. Add the brown sugar and stir until dissolved, then pour in the citrus juice and cognac, increase the heat to medium-high, and bring to a boil. Boil for 1 minute and then turn off the heat. Add the apples in an even layer and set aside.

Melt the remaining 8 tbsp/115 g butter in a microwave or small sauce-pan and set aside. Whisk together the flour, granulated sugar, baking powder, and salt in a large bowl. In a medium bowl, whisk the egg until it is very foamy, 1 to 1½ minutes. Whisk in the milk and vanilla, and then whisk in the melted butter.

Pour the liquid ingredients over the dry ingredients and whisk together until they're just combined. Pour the batter over the apples and place the frying pan in the oven. Bake until a cake tester inserted into the center of the cake comes out clean, about 25 minutes. Remove from the oven and let rest 5 for minutes. Run a paring knife around the edges of the cake. Place a rimmed plate or circular serving platter over the top of the cake (the plate should be a few inches wider than the pan to catch all of the caramel) and invert the cake onto the platter. Slice into wedges and serve.

VARIATION: PINEAPPLE UPSIDE-DOWN CAKE
Drain a 12-oz/340-g can of pineapple chunks, and use them in place of the apples.

FARM ✺ YARN

APPLES GALORE

In Washington County, fall desserts are all about showcasing apples (as you can tell from the many apple desserts in this chapter). Each October, our neighbors Judy and Ron DeWitt host an apple-pressing party at their home. It's an autumn tradition that I salivate for as soon as I start twisting apples off our trees. In the fall, they invite all the neighbors over to their beautifully restored home to turn Pippins, Northern Spys, and Cortlands (among other varieties) into the most delightfully spry and refreshing apple juice. It's so full of natural sweetness and pure apple flavor that once you taste it, you're spoiled forever.

We go to several orchards—including our own where Pippins hang low from the trees—for apples in the fall. Some, like Honeycrisps, we save for eating, while others, like Belle de Boskoop and Northern Spys are earmarked for pies, tarts, and apple butter. This is a short list of our favorite local apples and what we use them in the most.

Washington County Apples

BELLE DE BOSKOOP: Aromatic and perfumed, this is an apple that is lovely in tarts and pies, as well as in apple butter.

CORTLAND: A slightly tart New York native that resists discoloring after slicing. Like the Northern Spy, this is a great apple for pies and crisps.

FORTUNE: Rich and spicy; we like to eat these raw and add them to salads.

GINGER GOLD: A late-summer apple with a slightly spicy flavor. Very nice in pies, tarts, and the Spiced Rhubarb Jam on page 63.

HONEYCRISP: Supercrisp, juicy, and sweet. Our favorite eating apple.

MUTSU (CRISPIN): Nice, crisp, and with a slightly spicy flavor, it's a good pie apple.

NORTHERN SPY: Another apple indigenous to New York. Known as the best apple for pies because the slices keep their shape, even after baking.

PIPPINS: Tender, firm, crisp, and juicy; another great apple for baking and for making apple butter.

RHODE ISLAND GREENING: Extra-tart and juicy. Great in pies (use instead of Granny Smith apples) and just about anything.

WINESAP: Extra-firm with a beautifully deep red skin. Lovely with cheese and in salads.

RUSTIC DOUBLE APPLE TART

*This free-form rustic tart showcases apples in two ways: first, with a cush-
ion of long-cooked and silken apple butter, and second, with a top layer of
crisp fall apples that are sliced extra thin so they absolutely melt in your
mouth when you eat them. My tart dough takes on an incredible yellow
color thanks to egg yolks from the girls in the barn and Kerrygold butter
from Ireland. Simple, rustic, and delicious, an apple tart is one of my
staples for fall dinner parties.*

To make the pastry: Slice the butter into small pieces, place them in a
bowl, and put in the freezer to chill. Pulse together the flour and salt.
Whisk the egg yolk with the cold water and set aside. Add the cold
butter to the flour mixture and pulse until the dry ingredients are mealy
with nuggets no larger than a small pea. Pulse in the liquid just until
the dry ingredients look sandy and then turn the mixture out onto
your worksurface. Bring the dry ingredients together with your hands,
kneading lightly until it can be pressed into a mound (if you tap it, it
should break apart). Transfer the mound to a large sheet of plastic wrap,
wrap it tightly, and lightly knead to make a solid, flat disc. Chill the
dough for at least 45 minutes or up to 3 days.

Heat the oven to 400°F/200°C/gas 6. Unwrap the dough and place it
on a generously floured worksurface. Roll it out to a 9½-in/24-cm circle.
Fold the dough into quarters and transfer it to an 11-by-18-in/28-by-
45-cm baking sheet. Sprinkle the top of the dough with the sugar and
continue to roll it on the baking sheet until it becomes a somewhat
roundish 12- to 13-in/30.5- to 33-cm rectangle.

To prepare the tart: Evenly spread the apple butter over the dough,
leaving a 3-in/7.5-cm perimeter at the edge. Peel, core, and halve the
apples, and then, using a mandolin or a sharp chef's knife, slice 3 apple
halves as thinly as possible, about ¹⁄₁₆ in/2 mm thick. Arrange half of
the sliced apples in concentric circles over the apple butter so that they
slightly overlap.

continued . . .

Serves 6

FOR THE PASTRY

6 tbsp/85 g unsalted butter

1⅔ cups/185 g all-purpose flour,
plus extra for rolling

¾ tsp kosher salt or fleur de sel

1 egg yolk

3 tbsp cold water

2 tbsp sugar

FOR THE TART

⅓ cup/80 g apple butter store-
bought or homemade (page 158)

2 tart, firm apples

1 tbsp unsalted butter, frozen

3 tsp sugar

1 tsp lemon zest

2 tbsp fresh lemon juice

3 tbsp cream or milk

Vanilla ice cream for serving

Using a mandolin or the large-hole side of a box grater, grate the butter into fine shavings. Sprinkle 1 tsp of the sugar over the apples and follow with half of the butter shavings, all the lemon zest, and 1 tbsp of the lemon juice. Layer the remaining apples over the first layer, sprinkle with 1 tsp sugar, all but a few pieces of the leftover butter, and the remaining 1 tbsp lemon juice. Cut the remaining apple half into ⅛-in-/3-mm-thick slices by hand, and then arrange decoratively over the top. Fold the edges of the dough up and over the apples, overlapping the dough as you work your way around the tart. Tuck the last few bits of butter into the apples. Brush the edges of the dough with the cream, and sprinkle with the remaining 1 tsp sugar.

Bake the tart until the apples are singed at their edges and the pastry is golden brown, 35 to 45 minutes. Let cool for at least 20 minutes before serving, preferably with a scoop of vanilla ice cream.

COGNAC-CURED FRUITCAKE

Makes 3 loaves

1 lb/455 g mixed dried and/or candied fruits (like apricots, candied citron, candied lemon peel, candied orange peel, candied or dried cherries, craisins, currants, dates, figs, and raisins)

8 oz/225 g mixed toasted nuts (like almonds, cashews, macadamia nuts, pecans, pine nuts, pistachios, and walnuts)

1¾ cups/420 ml cognac, plus more as needed

1¼ lbs/570 g plus 2 tbsp unsalted butter, at room temperature

5⅔ cups/720 g all-purpose flour, plus extra for dusting pans

¼ tsp ground cinnamon

¼ tsp ground cloves

¼ tsp ground ginger

¼ tsp ground nutmeg

1½ tsp baking powder

½ tsp salt

8 large eggs

1 orange, zested and juiced

1 tbsp dark or black-strap molasses

1 tbsp orange marmalade

¼ tsp vanilla extract

¼ tsp almond extract

¼ tsp orange flower water

1¼ cups/250 g light or dark brown sugar

1¼ cups/250 g granulated sugar

3 tbsp superfine sugar

One of my favorite childhood memories is actually a smell—the sweet, alcohol-laced fragrance of this incredible fruitcake made by Shashi Auntie, who lived next door to my family in New Delhi. Every November, she'd begin soaking dried and candied fruits in rum or brandy to make stacks and stacks of fruitcakes that would fill her house as the weeks progressed, all to be given away to friends and neighbors as Christmas gifts. When I moved to New York City, as soon as the temperature dropped and the leaves began to fall, I developed an insatiable craving for Shashi Auntie's fruitcake. I got her recipe and started baking them to give away to my friends and colleagues in my new home. Two of my closest friends, Nitin and Mamta, ate with such gusto that I decided to always have some on hand to offer as a treat when they visited. Wrapped in cognac-soaked muslin, dusted with superfine sugar, wrapped in plastic wrap and then aluminum foil, and stored in a snug airtight plastic container, the cake would last for up to a year so long as I replenished the cognac, sugar, and coverings every time I removed a slice or two. The longer it aged, the higher proof it became, making our visits evermore spirited as the year progressed!

Now that we live in the country, Shashi Auntie's fruitcake has become even more of a staple. Charlie and I start soaking the fruits in the fall so that come holiday time, we can make delightfully decadent high-spirited fruitcakes to eat, give, and serve throughout the season. This recipe yields three cakes: one to save, one to give, and one to sample! While we always use good cognac in our fruitcake, you can feel free to substitute less-expensive brandy or rum if you prefer.

❋ ❋ ❋

Place the dried fruits, nuts, and 1 cup/240 ml of the cognac in a bowl or 1-gl/3.8-L resealable plastic bag. Set aside at room temperature for at least 1 week or up to several months (continue to top off the amount of cognac so the fruits continue to sweeten in the alcohol).

Heat the oven to 350°F/180°C/gas 4. Grease three 5-by-9-in/14-by-23-cm loaf pans with 1 tbsp butter each. Add 2 tbsp flour to each pan, and shake to coat the bottoms and sides. Set aside.

Whisk together the flour, cinnamon, cloves, ginger, nutmeg, baking powder, and salt in a large bowl and set aside. In another large bowl, whisk the eggs with the orange zest and juice, molasses, marmalade, vanilla, almond extract, and orange flower water and set aside.

Beat the remaining butter with the brown sugar and granulated sugar in a stand mixer (or in a large bowl if using a hand mixer) on low speed until combined. Increase the speed to medium-high and beat until light and creamy, about 2 minutes. Reduce the speed to low. Add one-third of the flour mixture, followed by half of the egg mixture. Repeat, ending with the last one-third of the flour mixture, scraping the bowl between additions as necessary. Mix in the cognac-soaked fruit and nuts (leave any excess liquid behind), and then scrape the batter into the prepared pans.

Place the pans in the oven, and bake for 1 hour. Rotate the pans, reduce the heat to 300°F/150°C/gas 2, and continue to bake until a cake tester inserted into the center of each cake comes out clean and the center of each resists light pressure, about 30 minutes longer. Check occasionally—if the cakes look like they are browning too quickly, loosely tent with aluminum foil. Remove the cakes from the oven, and let cool completely in the pans.

Place three large pieces of muslin (large enough to completely wrap around each cake; you can also use several layers of cheesecloth in place of muslin) in a bowl and pour the remaining ¾ cup/180 ml cognac over it. Run a paring knife around the edges of each pan to loosen the cakes. Turn each cake out onto a plate. Wrap the cognac-soaked muslin around the cakes so all surfaces, edges, and sides are covered. Sprinkle the top of the cakes with superfine sugar, and then wrap tightly in plastic wrap followed by a layer of aluminum foil. Let the cakes cure in the refrigerator for 1 week (or up to 1 year). Before serving, let the cake sit out at room temperature for 30 minutes before slicing.

RECIPE NOTE

Every time you remove a slice, resoak the muslin in ¼ cup/60 ml fresh cognac, sprinkle with another 3 tbsp sugar, and rewrap in fresh sheets of plastic wrap and aluminum foil. If storing for more than 1 week, be sure to soak and replace the muslin on a weekly basis.

UPSTATE APPLE BUTTER

Makes six 1-pt/475-ml jars

3 cinnamon sticks

I tsp whole cloves

I tsp whole green cardamom pods

½ tsp whole black peppercorns

½ tsp fennel seeds

¼ tsp anise seeds

1-in/2.5-cm piece ginger, peeled and roughly chopped

10 lb/4.5 kg apples (about 32 apples), preferably a mix of tart, sweet, and slightly acidic varieties (see page 152), peeled, cored, and roughly chopped

4 cups/960 ml apple cider

5 cups/1 kg sugar

In upstate New York, we are blessed with a multitude of apple orchards, many of which are reintroducing heirloom apples to the public. It's amazing to discover and taste the various varieties and expand our apple repertoire. Belle de Boskoop is a variety that was new to me—I love it for its incredibly aromatic contribution to apple butter and sauce. I get them from fifth-generation family-run Saratoga Apple in Schuylerville, New York. My other two favorite varieties for cooking and baking are Northern Spys and Rhode Island Greenings, both early American cultivars that I buy from Hicks Orchard in Granville, the oldest u-pick in New York (since 1905). While the Northern Spy is juicy and crisp, Rhode Island Greenings contribute a wonderful tartness. Used in combination, these three little-known varieties lend our apple butter great flavor and history. Unless you have a spare freezer or refrigerator in a cellar or garage, you may choose to cook a half batch of this recipe.

❀ ❀ ❀

Place the cinnamon, cloves, cardamom, peppercorns, fennel seeds, anise, and ginger in a large square of cheesecloth. Gather the four corners together, tie with butcher's twine, and place in a large stockpot. Add the apples and apple cider and bring to a hard simmer over medium-high heat. Reduce the heat to medium-low and simmer gently, stirring often, until the apples easily mash against the sides of the pot, about 1 hour.

Remove the spice sachet from the pot and save to use later. Fill a blender about halfway with the apple mixture and purée until completely smooth (alternatively an immersion blender is perfect for this kind of job). Transfer the apple purée to a clean pot and repeat with the remaining apples and liquid.

Return the spice sachet to the apple purée and stir in the sugar. Bring to a boil, reduce the heat to medium, and gently simmer, stirring occasionally, until the mixture is thick, 1 hour to 1 hour and 15 minutes (if the apple butter starts to splatter, reduce the heat).

Remove and discard the spice sachet. If you plan on canning the apple butter, ladle the hot mixture into sterilized jars following the instructions below. Or let the apple butter cool to room temperature, and then refrigerate for up to 3 weeks or freeze for up to 6 months.

RECIPE NOTE: CANNING CHUTNEY, JAM, AND FRUIT BUTTER

Even when I lived in a cramped Manhattan apartment, I always found the space (and time) to can jams, chutneys, and fruit butters. The process is simple—just make sure you have the right supplies on hand before beginning. Wash canning jars, lids, and bands in hot soapy water and rinse well. Place the jars and bands (not the lids) in a large pot and cover with 2 in/5 cm of water. Bring to a boil, cover, reduce the heat slightly, and gently boil for 10 minutes (or place them in the top rack of the dishwasher and run them through a cycle). Remove the jars and bands using tongs and place upside down on a clean kitchen towel to drain.

Fill the jars with hot jam, jelly, or fruit butter (a funnel is very handy for this job), leaving a ¼-in/6-mm headspace at the top. Wipe off the rims with a clean towel, place the lids on the jars, and seal. Place the filled jars on a canning rack in a deep canning pot or stockpot and cover with water. Bring to a boil, cover, and boil for 10 minutes. Remove the jars from the pot using tongs and place them on a kitchen towel to cool (you may hear the lids pop as they seal—this is a good thing!) completely. Before storing, press the top of the lid to make sure it doesn't bounce back—this means the lid is properly sealed. If it does bounce back, repeat the boiling process.

Canning Checkist

- Canning pot
- Canning rack
- Clean kitchen towels
- Funnel
- Jar lifter
- Jars, lids, bands
- Permanent marker and/or stickers for labeling contents, as well as noting the date (month/year)
- Tongs

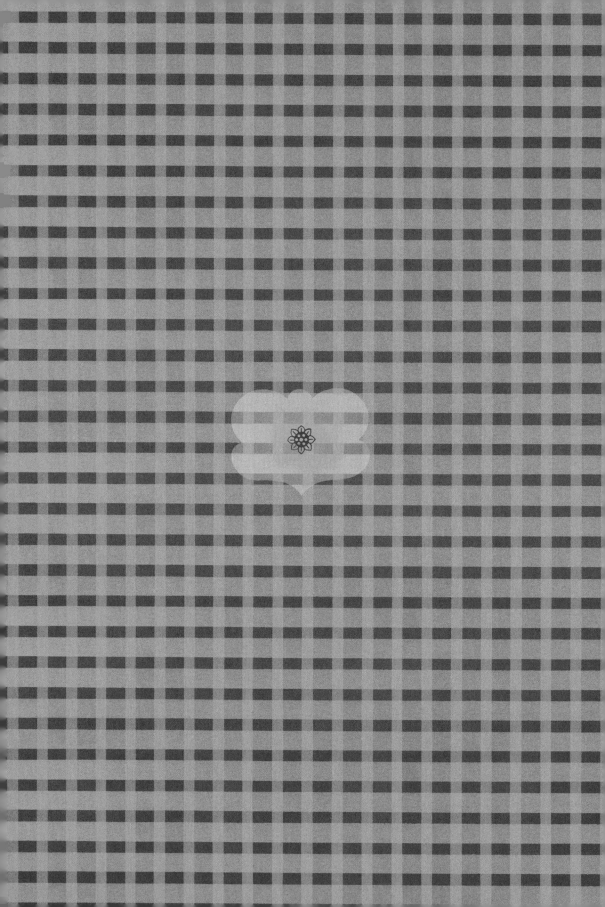

CHAPTER FOUR

WINTER

❀

A Rekindling of Community

The long, harsh, and challenging winter is also the time of year when the true spirit of the North Country people shines. Hearths fill with the sound of crackling wood fires, the air is crisp, and the tables are set for lots of cold-weather entertaining. During what seems like a never-ending season of snow and plummeting temperatures is actually the time of year we look forward to the most—because it's when nearly all of us can slow down and rekindle relationships with each other. After moving to the farm, Charlie and I learned quickly that the verdant spring and summer months are lovely, fall is magical, and winter is really where the heart of our community lies.

While some may think that winter and its harsh, bleak-colored reality of whites, grays, and browns (with an occasional shock of piercing blue sky) might rob locals of joy and happiness, the contrary is true. During the frigid months that make summer seem a million years away, friends and neighbors quickly fill our calendar with brunch and dinner invitations. They open their homes and fire up their hearths, and we gather together around comforting fireplaces to catch up on the season past and the seasons ahead.

Our immediate neighbors, Joe and Sally Brillon, have a wood-fired hearth that dates to the 1840s, and it was there that I spent my first country Thanksgiving and experienced the ease and graciousness of rural hospitality. A turkey slowly roasted over the open fire and other casseroles and side dishes were cooked in the natural heat of the hearth. Homemade hummus, baba ghanoush, and even pita bread were served. I realized that my new neighbors did not fit any country stereotype I could have dreamed up—and they realized the same about me.

As free as the animals are during the warm months of the year, during the colder times they remind us of our responsibilities and duties toward their survival. Charlie and I are out in the snow, sleet, and freezing rain every morning and night filling water containers for the goats and chickens; heaving bales of hay and back-breaking bags of feed from one barn to another, and providing general company and comfort to the geese and ducks who expect nothing yet are so delighted to find grain and interaction in the stark winter.

After being outside in the elements, nothing beats retreating to the sofa in front of a stoked fire with a cup of hot chai and maybe some spicy Indian snacks or a tea biscuit to take off the chill. Charlie reads his farming manuals, and I knit or crochet—we are quite the picture, the two of us, a new representation of American Gothic if ever there was one. The wind howls through the barren trees, the sky grows dark, and a quiet like you've never experienced before takes over the farm. It is eerie and beautiful and incredibly serene. I don't find myself missing the frenetic energy of Manhattan for one second.

Of course, the warm kitchen is where we spend most of our time in the winter. The perfume of a Kerala-style onion and egg roast or a cranberry-strawberry galette just out of the oven fills our home with a cozy fragrance no jar of potpourri could hope to duplicate. We cook and create new recipes and have fun rummaging through our larder, using up jars of jam preserved in the summer, or unique vinegars, seasonings, and dried fruits and mushrooms purchased on trips abroad. Friends come by for dinner, congregating at the kitchen island, and we often never even make it to the dining table, eating up the delicious food as I cook it. Samosas, dumplings, soups, and roasts are served alongside conversations about politics, religion, or just plain country gossip. It's all a part of the winter table, providing us with sustenance and stories to see us through until spring.

OLD-FASHIONED EGGNOG

Serves 8 to 10

4 cups/950 ml milk

9 large eggs

1⅓ cups/265 g sugar

¼ tsp kosher salt

3 cups/720 ml heavy cream

⅓ cup/80 ml Grand Marnier

⅓ cup/80 ml cognac or bourbon

¾ tsp vanilla bean paste, or
1¼ tsp vanilla extract

Freshly grated nutmeg

There is nothing quite like lusciously silky, rich, and creamy eggnog during the holidays. It couldn't be simpler to make, yet the art of homemade eggnog has fallen by the wayside, with convenient store-bought cartons laden with artificial ingredients, preservatives, and nasty thickeners taking its place. Make this once and you'll be amazed—I have served it to fine chefs, city slickers, and country friends alike, and all are always charmed by its pureness and wonderfully luxurious texture. Make eggnog with the freshest eggs you can find and be prepared to rediscover the charms of this delicious holiday tradition.

❄ ❄ ❄

Bring the milk to a boil in a large saucepan and turn off the heat.

Crack the eggs into a large bowl and whisk in the sugar, then slowly pour in the hot milk while whisking constantly. Return the mixture to the saucepan, add the salt, and cook over low heat until it coats the back of a wooden spoon (your finger should leave a trail that doesn't run) and it reads 170°F/77°C on an instant-read thermometer, 6 to 8 minutes.

Pour the eggnog base through a fine-mesh sieve and into a large bowl. Stir in 2⅔ cups/640 ml of the cream, the Grand Marnier, cognac, and vanilla. Cover with plastic wrap and chill until cold.

Before serving, in a medium bowl, whip the remaining ⅓ cup/80 ml cream to soft peaks. Whisk the whipped cream into the eggnog and serve with a pinch of nutmeg.

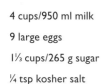

FARM ❀ YARN

EBAY FOR EGGS

Maricel Presilla, a dear friend, chef, and businesswoman with two successful restaurants in Hoboken, visited us at the farm during our first summer here. The whole time she was with us, she kept saying the same thing—that we absolutely must get some Penedesenca chickens, since they lay the most beautiful dark-chocolate-brown eggs. If anyone understands my motives when it comes to chickens, it's Maricel. While many farmers might have chickens for purely practical reasons—like to provide meat and eggs—Maricel and I have them for idealistic reasons. We have chickens because we love everything about them, from how the chicks follow the mother hen to their beautiful plumage to their cautious curiosty. At Maricel's urging, I visited Egg-Bid.com, a Web site selling every kind of heritage chicken you can imagine. Just like on eBay, people bid against one another for rare eggs, from Penedesencas to Polish and everything in between. Needless to say, I got hooked, and a couple of afternoons later, we had a dozen or so chicks of various pedigree and breed arrive via FedEx!

Because I have a fascination with all kinds of birds, I didn't stop at chickens. I ordered guinea hens, wood ducks, and even Chinese Ringneck pheasants. The males of both species of pheasants and ducks are phenomenal to look at, like living art. I had to have them!

One morning, eight boxes arrived. Charlie took the boxes to an open-roof area of the barn that had bedding and was separate from the other animals. He stirred some sugar into water, as he planned to feed them as soon as they were let out of the boxes (the birds are often a bit stressed and need liquid and electrolytes). Charlie opened the top flaps of the boxes, and *whoosh*—just like that, all but two birds flew away! Nine hundred dollars was gone in seconds! (We hadn't realized that, unlike chickens who are shipped as small baby chicks only able to skit around, pheasants and ducks arrive as juveniles, about one year old.)

My mother happened to be visiting from India, and she and Charlie ran into the fields hopping after the pheasants, trying to catch them. It was a hysterical sight! A few days later, our neighbor Sally Longo (of Sally's Veggie Dumplings with Ginger-Soy Dipping Sauce fame, page 176) asked us what to do with a gorgeous and wounded Ringneck pheasant that she found on her property. We were delighted to discover the location of one of the birds but devastated to hear of its injury. Charlie and Mom brought the pheasant home and, combined with the two that we managed to keep on the property, we had a whole pheasant family. But we realized that pheasants are much happier wild than in capitivity, so we ended up letting them all loose, and now whenever neighbors spot the gorgeous birds in the countryside, they report back to us. It makes us happy to know that we inadvertently beautified the area with these incredible birds.

As for the wood ducks, they come to our pond every day throughout the spring. From the initial four that flew the coop grew a family of ten to twelve ducks. We watch them bathe and play in the pond and fly off to the woods that flank our property. It is the best of both worlds really—they get to enjoy the wild and we get to enjoy their beauty, albeit unpredictable and fleeting.

FARMHOUSE CHAI

Serves 4 to 6

2 cups/480 ml milk

1 cup/240 ml water

1½ tbsp loose-leaf black tea, like Darjeeling, Nilgiri, or Assam

10 whole green cardamom pods, lightly crushed to break open the pods

6 whole black peppercorns

6 whole cloves

2-in/5-cm piece fresh ginger, peeled and roughly chopped

1½-in/3.75-cm cinnamon stick, broken in half

1 tbsp sugar

In India, chai is just part of the day—you wake up; you have chai. While the drinking of tea in Western countries comes with a lot of pomp and circumstance—tea cozies, strainers, fine teapots—in India, chai, made from black tea leaves, spices, milk, water, and a bit of sugar, is an ordinary thing people of all backgrounds and lifestyles drink throughout the day and without much fanfare. It's not as caffeinated as coffee, so you can drink more of it, and it's available everywhere, often alongside bread pakoras sold by street vendors.

American chai is nothing like Indian chai. While this beverage in India is balanced and nuanced—the sweetness of the cardamom and cinnamon is tempered by the astringency of the ginger, the heat of the clove, and a touch of spice from black peppercorns—domestic chai is often candy sweet and horribly spiced, with too much cinnamon or overwhelming amounts of cloves. My chai is neither cloyingly sweet nor overly spiced. I boil it for fifteen minutes to bring out the tannins in the tea, but if you like a softer flavor, do not boil it as long (in India, people boil it even longer than fifteen minutes). My favorite loose-leaf tea to use is the Darjeeling I buy from Chaiwalla in Connecticut—it's delicate and soft, and allows the flavors of the spices to come through. For a stronger tea try Nilgiri; Assam (Charlie's favorite) delivers the most assertive cup of chai.

✽ ✽ ✽

Place the milk and water in a medium saucepan. Add the tea, cardamom, peppercorns, cloves, ginger, cinnamon, and sugar and bring to a boil over medium-high heat. Turn off the heat, cover the pan, and steep for 15 minutes. Remove the lid and turn the heat to high. Once the chai returns to a boil, take it off the heat and pour it through a fine-mesh sieve and into glasses (not teacups). Serve hot.

BUTTERNUT SQUASH CHAAT

On frigid, snowy days, it doesn't hurt to have a root cellar full of winter squash just waiting to be used. This is a quick-to-make dish that is delicious on its own, alongside a pork chop or roasted chicken, or eaten with eggs for breakfast. You may also use a combination of root vegetables, including celeriac, parsnips, and rutabaga.

❊ ❊ ❊

Preheat the oven to 375°F/190°C/gas 5. Place the squash cubes in a large baking dish and toss with the canola oil and 1 tsp of the salt. Roast until the squash is tender and browned around the edges, 45 minutes to 1 hour, stirring every 20 minutes.

Transfer the hot squash to a large bowl and add the remaining ½ tsp salt, toasted cumin, *chaat* masala, and cayenne. Squeeze the limes over the squash. Serve warm or at room temperature.

Serves 4 to 6

One 2½-lb/1.2-kg butternut squash, peeled, halved, seeded, and diced into 1-in/2.5-cm cubes

1½ tbsp canola or grapeseed oil

1½ tsp kosher salt

1 tbsp Toasted Cumin (page 221)

¼ tsp *chaat* masala (see page 214)

⅛ to ¼ tsp cayenne pepper

2 limes, halved

BUTTERNUT SQUASH, APPLE, AND CRANBERRY GRATIN

We have squash in spades throughout the winter months, and I'm always looking for new ways to prepare it. I never thought about serving it with sweet apples and sweet-tart cranberries, but after trying a version prepared by the chefs at Yale during a dinner celebrating Indian food, I was hooked on the balance between creamy and chewy, sweet and spicy. It is a beautiful holiday side dish that I now prepare throughout the season. Most supermarkets sell squash already chopped into pieces. This is a great time-saver, since all of the peeling, seeding, and chopping is already done for you.

❋ ❋ ❋

Preheat the oven to 350°F/180°C/gas 4. Grease a 9-by-11-in/23-by-27-cm baking dish with the 1 tbsp room-temperature butter and set aside.

In a large bowl, toss together the squash, apples, cranberries, parsley, thyme, salt, pepper, and cayenne. Drizzle in the melted butter and stir to combine. Add the flour and mix to evenly coat the squash mixture.

Turn the mixture into the prepared baking dish and bake until the top is golden brown and the squash is tender but not mushy (a paring knife should easily slip into the center of a piece of squash), 45 to 50 minutes. Remove from the oven and let cool for 5 minutes before serving.

Serves 6

8 tbsp/115 g unsalted butter, melted, plus 1 tbsp at room temperature

One 3-lb/1.4-kg butternut squash, peeled, halved, seeded, and diced into 1-in/2.5-cm cubes

3 sweet-tart apples that will keep their shape after baking (see page 152), peeled, cored, and diced into ½-in/12-mm cubes

1⅓ cups/160 g dried cranberries

¼ cup/10 g finely chopped fresh flat-leaf parsley

½ tsp finely chopped fresh thyme

1 tbsp kosher salt

1 tsp freshly ground black pepper

¼ tsp cayenne pepper

1 heaping cup/140 g all-purpose flour

SWEET AND SOUR BUTTERNUT SQUASH

Serves 4 to 6

One 2¼- to 2½-lb/1- to 1.2-kg butternut squash

4 tbsp/60 ml canola or grapeseed oil

2-in/5-cm piece fresh ginger, peeled and minced

1 jalapeño, chopped

½ tsp cumin seeds

¼ tsp cayenne pepper

1½ tsp salt, plus extra if needed

1½ tsp sugar

Juice of ½ lime

When we moved to the farm, our next-door neighbors gave us a birdhouse housewarming gift that their sons had made out of a hollowed-out and dried butternut squash. It was so thoughtful and touching that when I was planning the vegetable garden, butternut squash was one of the first must-haves that came to mind.

❊ ❊ ❊

Cut the squash in half lengthwise. Peel it with a vegetable peeler or paring knife and scrape out the seeds. Cut the halves lengthwise into ½-in-/12-mm-thick strips. Then cut the strips crosswise into 1½-in/4-cm pieces.

Heat the canola oil in a large wok or frying pan over medium-high heat. Add the ginger and cook, stirring, for 1 minute. Add the jalapeño and cumin seeds and cook for 1 minute. Add the cayenne and cook, stirring, for 30 seconds.

Add the squash and stir to coat with the oil. Stir in the salt and sugar. Turn down the heat to medium. Cover and cook until the squash is tender, about 25 minutes. Uncover, stir the squash every 5 minutes, and check on the cooking; if the spices begin to burn, turn down the heat. If the squash doesn't brown at all, turn up the heat slightly.

Stir in the lime juice. Mash the squash with a spoon to break up some of the pieces. Season with salt and serve hot.

VARIATION: BUTTERNUT SQUASH FRITTATA

This is a great way to use leftover butternut squash. Preheat the oven to 400°F/200°C/gas 6. Whisk 8 large eggs with some chopped fresh cilantro, a pinch of cayenne, kosher salt, and ground black pepper and set aside. Melt 1 tbsp butter or warm 1 tbsp olive oil in a large oven-safe frying pan over medium-high heat. Add the squash and use a heatproof rubber spatula to press it into an even layer. Reduce the heat to medium, pour the eggs over the squash, and let it cook until the eggs are set, 5 to 8 minutes. Transfer the frying pan to the oven and bake until the frittata rises like a soufflé and is browned on top, an additional 5 to 8 minutes. Slice into wedges and serve.

ROASTED
MANCHURIAN CAULIFLOWER

From day one at my restaurant in New York City, Manchurian Cauliflower has been a huge success. It's sweet and spicy, tender and satiny, and looks as sultry and seductive as cauliflower could ever hope to become. In the restaurant, we fry the cauliflower, toss it with the sauce, and finish it in the oven. Here I've simplified and lightened the recipe by roasting the cauli-flower and tossing it with sauce midway through baking. Healthier, easier, and more accessible, you could make a double batch of this recipe and still never have leftovers!

❁ ❁ ❁

Preheat your oven to 425°F/220°C/gas 7. Grease a 9-by-11-in/23-by-27-cm baking dish with 1½ tbsp of the canola oil and set aside.

Grind the cardamom, chiles (if using), coriander seeds, cumin seeds, and peppercorns in a coffee grinder or small food processor until fine. Mix the spices with the remaining 1½ tbsp oil in a large bowl. Add the cauliflower, sprinkle with the salt, and toss to coat. Transfer the vegetables to a baking dish and roast for 20 minutes.

To make the sauce: Heat the canola oil and pepper in a large frying pan over medium-high heat for 1 minute. Add the garlic and cook until fragrant, about 1 minute, stirring often. Add the ketchup and cook for 2 minutes, stirring occasionally. Reduce the heat to medium and add the cayenne and salt. Cook until the ketchup thickens and becomes deep red in color, stirring occasionally, 6 to 8 minutes.

When the cauliflower has roasted for 20 minutes, add the sauce to the pan and stir to evenly coat the cauliflower. Continue roasting until the cauliflower is tender, another 20 to 30 minutes, stirring midway through. Serve immediately.

Serves 8

3 tbsp canola or grapeseed oil

3 whole green cardamom pods

3 dried red chiles (optional)

1 tbsp coriander seeds

1 tsp cumin seeds

½ tsp whole peppercorns

One 2½- to 3-lb/1.2- to 1.4-kg head cauliflower, cored and broken into medium florets

1 tsp kosher salt

FOR THE SAUCE

2 tbsp canola or grapeseed oil

½ tsp freshly ground black peppercorns

8 garlic cloves, finely chopped

1½ cups/360 ml ketchup

½ tsp cayenne pepper

¼ tsp kosher salt

FARM ❀ YARN

GOOSE NUMBER 1,263

City slickers' and country folks' atti-
tudes are at polar opposites when it
comes to animals and death; and our
perspective changed irreversibly not
long after we moved onto the farm. My
parents were visiting from India, and
my sister, Seema, and her son and hus-
band were staying with us as well. In
addition to family, we had friends
in the guesthouse, so the mood was
celebratory and spirits were festive.

One crisp afternoon, the kind
when the sky is blue beyond what
seems natural and the air is tinged
with smoke and frost, we were all
out walking a circle around the pond.
Charlie counted twelve geese and
briefly wondered where the other two
had gone. We rounded the pond and
there, lying in the grass, was one
of our stunning Tufted Roman geese,
snowy white feathers stained with
blood and completely dismembered.
Before Charlie could react, I called
him over to a grassy area just off
the pond because I had found the other
missing goose. It was hissing at me,
which was strange because they usually only do that when they lay eggs.
Charlie ran over, still pale and out
of sorts from seeing the first mur-
dered goose. He picked the hissing
goose up off the ground, and the poor

thing had only one leg among other
gruesome inflictions too horrible to
relay. The sight made my stomach turn
and my eyes well with tears. Charlie
was shocked into silence.

We didn't know what to do. So we
did what we would have done at that
time for any other hurt animal—we took
it to the vet. While I consoled my
family and our guests (a dismembered
animal is not exactly the take-away
snapshot you want people leaving the
farm with), Charlie and our farmhand
wrapped the goose in a cashmere blanket and zipped down the road at warp
speed in our Mercedes wagon.

The vet took one look at the
bird and told Charlie that it wasn't
going to make it. He asked if Charlie
wanted to bring it home or have them
euthanize it. It was not a decision
we were prepared to make lightly; we
discussed it with my family, with our
guests, and over a civilized lunch,
of course. By the time we arrived at
the vet to relay our much-debated
decision, they informed us that it
had already been euthanized. The vet
asked if we wanted to have the goose
cremated with other birds and have
its ashes sprinkled over the "Field
of Eternity" or cremated privately
and delivered to us in an urn. I

mulled over what to do (thinking back
on this, I realize how silly it was,
of course—it wasn't a house pet but
a farm animal!). Charlie made the
decision for me—"I am not going to
have a room full of urns for all of
the deaths that will occur on the
farm!" he said. Field of Eternity it
would be.

A few weeks later, we received a
card from the vet conveying condo-
lences for goose number 1,263.

That was how we dealt with our
first animal death on the farm. A
$2.25 goose cost us $200 to cremate.
Now we don't bother with such hulla-
baloo if an animal is in agony and
injured. We deal with the wounded
creature on-site (a quick, humane
death administered by rifle and a
steady hand) and compost it as
nature intended.

SALLY'S VEGGIE DUMPLINGS WITH GINGER-SOY DIPPING SAUCE

Makes about 3 dozen dumplings

FOR THE DOUGH

2 cups/255 g all-purpose flour, plus extra for rolling

⅔ cup/160 ml boiling water

¼ cup/60 ml cold water

FOR THE FILLING

2 scallions, green and white parts, thinly sliced

I medium carrot, shredded

½ cup/35 g finely chopped cremini mushrooms

¼ cup/35 g thawed frozen corn kernels, drained

¼ small head/200 g cabbage, shredded

¼ cup/30 g peeled and diced jicama

¼ cup/4 g finely chopped fresh cilantro

I oz/25 g tofu, pressed between paper towels to absorb extra liquid, finely diced (¼ cup)

2-in/5-cm piece fresh ginger, grated

I habanero, finely minced (for less heat, substitute I jalapeño)

2 tbsp mirin (rice wine)

1½ tbsp soy sauce

I tbsp minced fresh chives

It's not easy living in the country with taste buds that crave the flavors of the world. While it is easier now to find Mexican, Thai, and Indian food in rural America than it was even a few years ago, sadly the flavors are not always an authentic interpretation of the country and culture. So Charlie and I have learned to turn to our pantry when we get a taste for something ethnically inspired. Our dear friend Sally Longo shares our sentiments. Sally also happens to be the proprietor of the most highly regarded catering outfit in the area, Aunt Sally's, which is known to offer some of the best food in these parts. So when she rings and says she's on her way with fixings for dumplings, Charlie and I eagerly await her arrival. Made with a very simple homemade dumpling dough, these will spoil you forever.

Sally often drops by with the mise en place for her famous dumplings all ready to go (not even a blizzard can derail her when she has dumplings on the brain!), and we'll gather around the kitchen island and form an assembly line—one of us rolls the dough, another fills and shapes the dumplings, and someone else cooks them up. While we always make enough with intentions of freezing some for later, we more often than not devour two batches worth in a single sitting, popping them in our mouths as soon as they come out of the frying pan. Eating too many of Sally's crisp-bottomed, tender-steamed dumplings in a sitting is a food vice I am happy to succumb to. Blizzards, frigid temperatures, and even the fear of losing power during a wicked ice storm simply fade away when we come together to make dumplings, which always leads to lively conversation and much laughter. You can make these ahead and reheat them for two minutes in the microwave, but they're best eaten straightaway, hot from the frying pan.

❀ ❀ ❀

To make the dough: Place the flour in a large bowl and stir in the boiling water. Add the cold water and stir until a ball forms. Cover with plastic wrap and set aside to rest while you make the filling.

To make the filling: Fill a small bowl with water and place it next to your worksurface. Place the scallions, carrot, mushrooms, corn, cabbage, jicama, cilantro, tofu, ginger, habanero, mirin, soy sauce, chives, peanut butter, sugar, salt, sesame oil, and pepper in the bowl of a food processor and pulse three or four times, until the mixture is coarsely chopped and rough textured. Scrape the dumpling filling into a large bowl.

Generously flour your worksurface. Divide the dough into two equal halves, and place one half onto the floured worksurface. Flour the top of the dough and roll it into a ⅟₁₆-in-/2-mm-thick sheet (it shouldn't be so thin that you can see through it), lifting the dough occasionally to sprinkle flour beneath it if needed. Use a round 3-in/7.5-cm cookie cutter to stamp out 36 dough circles.

Place 1½ tsp of the filling in the center of each dough circle. Using your fingers or a pastry brush, moisten the bottom edge of each wrapper with water and fold the top half over the bottom so the edges meet. Press the edges together to seal them. Pick the dumpling up by the seam and rest it on your worksurface to create a flat bottom, and then pinch the edges together lightly to create a fluted edge (like a pie crust). Set each shaped dumpling on a parchment paper–lined baking sheet (don't let the dumplings touch one another—they will stick together). Repeat with the remaining dough and filling. Place in the freezer for at least 2 hours or up to 3 months (if freezing for longer than overnight, transfer the frozen dumplings to a resealable 1-gl/3.8-L freezer bag).

To make the dipping sauce: In a medium bowl, whisk together the soy sauce, water, sugar, lemon juice, mirin, balsamic vinegar, white wine vinegar, chile oil, and ginger. Add the scallion, cover with plastic wrap, and refrigerate.

Heat 2 tsp of the canola oil in a large frying pan over medium-high heat until it shimmers, 1 to 2 minutes. Remove the dumplings from the freezer and add half of them to the pan, cooking without moving them, until the bottoms are golden brown, 3 to 5 minutes (after 2 to 2½ minutes, use a spatula to peek under the dumplings and check the color). Pour ½ cup/ 120 ml of the water into the pan, reduce the heat to low, cover, and cook for 8 minutes. Use a spatula to transfer the dumplings to a platter. Cover with plastic wrap. Use paper towels to wipe out the moisture from the pan, and then begin the cooking process again. Serve hot with the dipping sauce on the side.

1 tbsp creamy peanut butter

1 tbsp sugar

½ tsp kosher salt

1 tsp toasted sesame oil

½ tsp freshly ground black pepper

1 cup/240 ml water

FOR THE DIPPING SAUCE

⅓ cup/80 ml soy sauce

⅓ cup/80 ml water

3 tbsp sugar

2 tbsp fresh lemon juice

1½ tsp mirin (rice wine)

1½ tsp balsamic vinegar

1½ tsp white wine vinegar

1½ tsp chile oil

1-in/2.5-cm piece fresh ginger, grated

1 scallion, root end trimmed, green and white parts thinly sliced

4 tsp canola or grapeseed oil

SHORTCUT POTATO AND PEA TURNOVERS

Makes 16 turnovers

FOR THE FILLING

2 lb/910 g red potatoes (about 6)

½ cup/8 g finely chopped fresh cilantro leaves

3 tbsp canola or grapeseed oil

2 dried red chiles, coarsely ground in a mortar and pestle

1 tbsp coriander seeds

2 tsp cumin seeds

⅛ tsp asafetida (see page 214)

¼ tsp cayenne pepper

2 tsp ground amchur (green mango powder)

1½ tsp kosher salt

¾ cup/100 g frozen peas

FOR THE TURNOVERS

1 large egg

1 tbsp water

⅛ tsp cayenne pepper

Pinch of kosher salt

All-purpose flour for rolling pastry

2 packages frozen puff pastry, thawed

Green Chutney (page 217) and/or Tamarind Chutney (page 219) for serving

When I was a young boy, Panditji, my family's longtime chef, would fry up hundreds of homemade samosas for Diwali, the Indian festival of light that occurs in the autumn. Anyone who ever ate Panditji's samosas would become instantly spoiled, never wanting anyone else's inferior version. The filling of his triangular turnovers had texture and roughness, while the homemade dough casing was as crisp and tender as you could imagine.

I have made a few concessions to allow me to fit samosas into my reality—instead of homemade dough, I use store-bought puff pastry, which saves me a ton of time. I also bake the turnovers instead of frying them, then serve as needed (you can even keep them warm in a 200°F/ 95°C oven for up to 30 minutes). These are excellent for serving as an appetizer, especially for large crowds, because they can be made in advance and frozen.

❈ ❈ ❈

To make the filling: Place the potatoes in a large pot, cover with 2 in/ 5 cm of water, and bring to a boil over high heat. Reduce the heat to a simmer and cook until a paring knife easily slips into the center of the longest potato, 15 to 20 minutes. Drain the potatoes and, once they're cool enough to handle, peel them, break them apart into crumbly pieces, and place in a large bowl. Stir in the cilantro and set aside.

Heat the canola oil with the ground red chiles, coriander seeds, cumin seeds, and asafetida in a large frying pan or wok over medium-high heat until the cumin is fragrant and golden brown, 1 to 2 minutes. Stir in the cayenne and then scrape in the potato mixture along with the amchur and salt. Stir in the peas and cook just until the potatoes and peas are warmed through, 3 to 4 minutes, stirring and scraping the bottom of the frying pan often to work in any browned bits. Transfer the mixture to a large bowl and set aside to cool completely.

To make the turnovers: Heat the oven to 400°F/200°C/gas 6. In a small bowl, whisk together the egg, water, cayenne, and salt, and set aside. Dust your worksurface with flour and place one sheet of puff pastry on top (if it came folded in thirds, keep it folded). Roll the folded pastry sheet to an approximate 8-by-13-in/20-by-33-cm rectangle. Starting 1 in/2.5 cm from the left edge, place 2 tbsp of the filling in the center of the pastry. Repeat three times, working your way across the pastry, leaving about 1½ in/4 cm between mounds and ending about 1 in/2.5 cm from the right edge.

Using a pastry brush, lightly paint the long edge of the pastry closest to you with the seasoned egg wash. Paint the left and right edges up to the midpoint of the pastry, and then paint between each of the mounds up to the middle of the pastry. Fold the top half of the pastry down over the bottom half, press the edges together to seal, and press the dough together in between each of the mounds. Trim the edges and cut between each mound so you have four turnovers. Press the tines of an upturned fork around the turnovers' edges to crimp. Brush with the egg wash and place on a baking sheet. Proceed with the remaining pastry and filling, making a dozen more turnovers. (The turnovers can be frozen on a baking sheet until they are hard, about 1 hour, and then transferred to a large resealable plastic bag and kept frozen for up to 3 months. Let the turnovers thaw before baking.) Bake the turnovers until golden brown, 15 to 20 minutes, rotating midway through cooking. Let cool for 10 minutes and serve warm or at room temperature with some chutney on the side.

COUNTRY RABBIT TERRINE WITH PISTACHIOS AND PERNOD

Sally Longo is one of our dearest North Country friends, and it is by her side that we've cooked so much amazing food at our farmhouse, including this rabbit terrine and the Rustic Rabbit Pâté with Juniper Berries on page 183, both elegant, inspired, and perfect for entertaining. The pistachios, fennel, and anise-y Pernod liqueur work pure magic in this terrine. Its refined and cosmopolitan flavor will have your guests wondering if you made this yourself or mail-ordered it from some fancy restaurant. If you're squeamish about removing the meat from the bone (in our house, that's Sally's job), ask your butcher to do it for you.

❄ ❄ ❄

Preheat the oven to 350°F/180°C/gas 4. Place a 5-by-9-in/12-by-23-cm loaf pan on the worksurface and place the bacon slices widthwise across the pan, slightly overlapping, so that the bacon covers the bottom and sides of the pan.

Set the rabbit on a cutting board and use a boning knife to slice away the meat from the bone, and then the sinew from the meat. Chop the meat into small cubes and then finely chop the liver.

Place the shallots and the Herbes de Hebron in a food processor and pulse together until the shallots are finely chopped. Add the liver, pulse to combine, and then add the rabbit meat and pulse until finely chopped with no pieces larger than ¼ in/6 mm, scraping the sides and bottom of the bowl as necessary.

In a large bowl, whisk together the egg, olive oil, Pernod, salt, and pepper. Add the fennel and the sausage and mix with your hands until the mixture is smooth. Use a rubber spatula to scrap the rabbit mixture into the egg mixture. Stir together and then fold in the pistachios, mixing well to combine.

continued . . .

Makes one 5-by-9-in/12-by-23-cm terrine

6 thin-cut fatty bacon slices

One 2½-lb/1.2-kg rabbit, liver reserved (save the heart and kidneys to make the Rustic Rabbit Pâté with Juniper Berries)

3 shallots, finely chopped

1 tbsp Herbes de Hebron (page 215) or herbes de Provence

1 large egg

2 tbsp extra-virgin olive oil

2 tbsp Pernod liqueur

1 tsp kosher salt

1 tsp freshly ground black pepper

1 fennel bulb, thinly shaved using a mandolin or vegetable peeler, feathery fronds reserved

1 lb/455 g mild pork sausage, squeezed out from its casing

2 cups/230 g toasted pistachios roughly chopped

Crackers or crusty bread for serving

Scrape the mixture into the prepared loaf pan and press and smooth out the top. Fold any bacon ends that hang out of the pan up and over the top of the terrine. Cover the top with a sheet of aluminum foil, crimping it around the edges to seal, and bake until an instant-read thermometer inserted into the center of the terrine reads 160°F/70°C, about 1 hour and 30 minutes.

Remove the terrine from the oven and set it on a cutting board. Loosen the foil slightly and then place a second same-size loaf pan on top of the foil. Place three cans of beans (or cans of tomatoes) in the loaf pan to weigh it down and set it aside for 2 to 3 hours to cool and compress. Remove the cans and loaf pan, and cover the terrine with plastic wrap. Refrigerate the terrine for at least 2 days or up to 1 week to allow the flavors to come together.

Before serving, place the loaf pan over a burner set to medium-high heat (to loosen the fat in the bottom of the pan). Run a paring knife around the edges of the terrine to loosen it from the pan and then invert it onto a serving platter. Garnish with the reserved fennel fronds and let the terrine sit out at room temperature for 10 minutes before serving with crackers or crusty bread.

RUSTIC RABBIT PÂTÉ WITH JUNIPER BERRIES

Along with the Country Rabbit Terrine with Pistachios and Pernod on page 181, this pâté often finds its way onto our holiday table. It's simultaneously beautiful, chic, and country—not just because pâté is so effortlessly elegant, but because it makes good use of leftover offal from the rabbit used to make the terrine. Don't be afraid of using ingredients like the heart, kidneys, and liver. Putting a whole animal to good use in the kitchen is smart and savvy, yielding absolutely delicious dishes that you can feel respectable serving. It's satisfying to know that when I make these two party-pleasing appetizers, I'm not wasting a single speck of the rabbit. In fact, you can even use the bones for stock (see Herbed Pheasant Breasts with Spiced Pomegranate Reduction, page 136, and Rabbit Stew with Porcini and Picholines, page 145).

❀ ❀ ❀

Using a mortar and pestle, grind together the juniper berries, salt, and peppercorns and set aside.

Melt the butter in a large frying pan over medium heat. Once melted, add the shallots, garlic, and thyme and cook just until the shallots are golden and becoming brown around the edges, 3 to 4 minutes. Add the hearts, livers, and kidneys and cook, stirring occasionally, until the livers are still slightly pink on the inside, 10 to 12 minutes. Turn off the heat and scrape the mixture into a food processor. Pour in the gin, add the juniper mixture, and pulse until mostly smooth but not pasty.

Use a rubber spatula to scrape the mixture into a 12-oz/355-ml ramekin. Cover tightly with plastic wrap and chill for at least 2 days or up to 1 week. Let the pâté sit at room temperature for 20 minutes before serving with baguette slices.

Serves 10 to 12

1 tsp juniper berries

1 tsp kosher salt

½ tsp freshly ground green peppercorns

8 tbsp/115 g unsalted butter

2 shallots, finely chopped

2 garlic cloves, finely chopped

1 tbsp fresh thyme, finely chopped

2 rabbit hearts

2 rabbit livers

2 sets rabbit kidneys (4 total)

1 tbsp gin

1 baguette, thinly sliced and toasted, for serving

NEW YEAR'S
BLACK-EYED PEA CURRY

Serves 6

¼ cup/60 ml canola or grapeseed oil

8 whole green cardamom pods

6 whole cloves

3 whole dried red chiles

2 bay leaves

1-in/2.5-cm cinnamon stick

½ tsp freshly ground black pepper

½ tsp whole cumin seeds

1½-in/4-cm piece fresh ginger, peeled and grated

1 large red onion, finely chopped

1 tbsp kosher salt, plus extra if needed

3 medium tomatoes, quartered

2 garlic cloves, finely minced or pressed through a garlic press

1 tbsp ground coriander

1 tsp ground cumin

1 tsp ground turmeric

½ tsp cayenne pepper

¼ cup/60 ml plain yogurt

Three 15 ½-oz/445-g cans black-eyed peas, rinsed and drained

½ tsp Garam Masala (page 216)

1 cup/240 ml water

Throughout the Southern states of America, black-eyed peas are served for good luck on New Year's Day. They're excellent with stir-fried cabbage— also considered a good-luck food, since it supposedly represents folded currency—and rice, of course (in the South, this dish would be called Hoppin' John). In India, my family's recipe for rongee, *Hindi for "black-eyed peas," is just as tasty. I often make it for our grand New Year's Eve celebration, happily knowing that the dish will probably be outshined by its fancier table competition, like crown roast of pork, Masala Chateaubriand (page 200), or a* biryani *rice dish. We pull out the good china and the sparkling stemware, load the wine cabinet with bubbly, and trim the house with glittering baubles, like three-foot-tall glass hurricanes filled with beautiful colored glass and twinkling holiday lights strung around the mantel and into antique bird cages. Our holiday tree (purchased from a nearby farm) is lavished with ornaments collected from around the world. It is a night we look forward to with great anticipation all year long, and any leftovers make New Year's Day that much tastier!*

❀ ❀ ❀

Heat the canola oil with the cardamom, cloves, chiles, bay leaves, cinnamon, pepper, and cumin seeds in a large heavy-bottomed pot over medium-high heat until the spices are fragrant, 1 to 2 minutes. Stir in the ginger and cook until it becomes fragrant and sticky, about 1 minute. Add the onion and salt and cook, stirring often, until the onion turns deeply browned and sticky, 15 to 20 minutes. If the onion begins to stick to the bottom of the pot or begins to burn, reduce the heat to medium and splash the pan with a bit of water, scraping up the browned bits and stirring them into the onion.

While the onion browns, place the tomatoes in a blender or food processor and purée until they are completely smooth. Set aside.

continued . . .

Stir the garlic into the onion mixture and cook until fragrant, 30 seconds to 1 minute. Add the coriander, ground cumin, and turmeric and cook until they begin to smell toasty, about 30 seconds. Stir in the cayenne and 2 tbsp of the yogurt. Cook until heated through, about 1 minute, and then add the remaining yogurt. Continue to stir and cook the yogurt and spices until the contents of the pot are thick and sticky and the liquid from the yogurt has evaporated, about 2 minutes. Stir in the tomato purée and bring to a boil. Reduce the heat to medium-low and cook until a film of oil pools on the surface of the sauce, 6 to 8 minutes.

Stir the black-eyed peas, garam masala, and water into the tomato mixture. Increase the heat to medium and cook, stirring often, until a bubble or two breaks at the surface, 5 to 7 minutes. Season with salt and serve hot.

FARM ❁ YARN

THE THREE FACES OF CURRY

Students, friends, and associates often ask me what the biggest misconception is when it comes to Indian food. Is it that it's rife with heat from chiles (actually no, there are entire regions of India where chiles are hardly ever used), or loaded with fat from frying (most Indian food is quite healthful, based on legumes, vegetables, and very little meat)? My answer is always this: curry.

There are three ways to define "curry" in India. The first is as a way of categorizing a type of dish that is saucy, like *gosht korma* (lamb curry) or *methi murgh* (chicken curry), though there isn't one dish that is "curry"—curry is rather a genre of dishes. "Curry" also refers to small deep-green leaves that look like a cross between California bay leaves and lemon verbena but taste like neither. In fact, the bright, tangy, citrusy taste of curry leaves is a flavor not easily replaced by another herb or spice.

The third way of classifying curry is the kind most known but ironically the least used by Indians—as a powder. Curry powder is a premixed blend of spices often heavy in fenugreek (for that "curry" taste) and turmeric (for that "curry" color). In India, the closest thing to curry powder is *sambhaar* powder (see page 219) in the south and garam masala in the north, which many households make or have made fresh every few days following a time-honored top-secret recipe unique to their family.

I love having people over who say point-blank that they are not big fans of Indian food. Usually it is because they have a dislike of curry powder—funny, isn't it, that most Indians would wholeheartedly agree with them! So I'll whip up some beautiful food, using the freshest vegetables, spices, and herbs, and without any trace of curry powder. Not only do they change their tune and sing the praise of the dish, but they often ask for the recipe!

BIRBAL KEE KHITCHEREE

Serves 6

FOR THE TOPPING

6 to 8 cups/1.4 to 1.9 L peanut oil

1 large red onion, halved and thinly sliced

¼ cup/10 g finely chopped fresh cilantro

2-in/5-cm piece fresh ginger, peeled and thinly sliced into very thin matchsticks

1 jalapeño, finely minced (remove the seeds for less heat)

1 tbsp fresh lime juice

FOR THE KHITCHEREE

1 cup/190 g split and hulled mung dal

2 tbsp ghee or clarified butter (see page 216)

10 whole green cardamom pods

8 whole cloves

3 bay leaves

2-in/5-cm cinnamon stick

1 tsp Panch Phoran (page 218)

¾ tsp ground turmeric

⅛ tsp asafetida (see page 214)

1 cup/185 g basmati rice

½ medium head cauliflower, divided into very small florets

1 medium red potato, cut into ½-in/12-mm pieces

4 medium carrots, peeled and finely chopped

continued . . .

When craving comfort food, I most often dream of khitcheree. The vegetarian one-pot meal of lentils, rice, and vegetables is transported to another dimension via multiple layers of spices—every bite is a new discovery of tastes and textures. The dish includes Panch Phoran, a spice blend of whole cumin, fennel, and the wonderfully exotic, nutty flavor of nigella seeds that are gently fried in ghee or clarified butter with coriander and tomatoes, and then a second boost of spice from a ghee-bloomed blend of more cumin, some cayenne, and oniony asafetida. It is such an incredible dish that there is even a legend behind it: Hundreds of years ago in mid-fourteenth-century India, Birbal, a court official of Emperor Akbar, made a khitcheree that was so enchanting the emperor decided to make Birbal a Raja king! At our house, we like to say that if it's good enough for Akbar and Birbal, it's good enough for you. This dish is so lovely that I often serve it with nothing else except for some Raita (page 218) and perhaps crispy papadum on the side. Make the recipe a few times and then begin to play with the flavors and simplify it as you like. I promise you won't be disappointed.

❀ ❀ ❀

To make the topping: Heat the oil in a large Dutch oven or other heavy pot (use enough oil to fill the saucepan to a 2-in/5-cm depth) over medium-high heat until it reaches 350°F/180°C on an instant-read thermometer. Add the onion and fry until crisp and browned, about 2 minutes, turning the onion occasionally. Use a slotted spoon or frying spider to transfer the onion to a paper towel–lined plate and set aside. (The oil can be saved for another use, but first let it cool, then strain it through a fine-mesh sieve into an airtight container.)

In a small bowl stir together the cilantro, ginger, jalapeño, and lime juice and set aside.

To make the khitcheree: Place the mung dal in a large frying pan over medium heat and toast it until fragrant and lightly golden, 3 to 5 minutes. Transfer the dal to a large plate and set aside.

continued . . .

7 cups/1.65 L water

10-oz/280-g bag frozen peas

**FOR THE FIRST
TEMPERING OIL**

2 tbsp ghee or clarified butter
(see page 216)

½ tsp Panch Phoran (page 218)

½ large red onion, halved and
thinly sliced

1½ tbsp kosher salt

2 tsp ground coriander

2 large tomatoes, finely diced

⅛ tsp cayenne pepper

3 cups/750 ml water

**FOR THE SECOND
TEMPERING OIL**

2 tbsp ghee or clarified butter
(see page 216)

½ tsp cumin seeds

¼ tsp cayenne pepper

Pinch of asafetida (see page 214)

½ tsp Garam Masala (page 216)

Place the ghee, cardamom, cloves, bay leaves, cinnamon, panch phoran, turmeric, and asafetida into the same pan and roast over medium heat until the spices are fragrant, about 2 minutes.

Add the rice, toasted dal, cauliflower, potato, and carrots and cook until the rice becomes translucent and the cauliflower sweats, 3 to 5 minutes, stirring often. Pour in the 7 cups/1.65 L of water, increase the heat to high, and bring to a boil. Add the peas, bring back to a boil, reduce the heat to medium-low, cover, and simmer for 20 minutes.

To make the first tempering oil: Heat the ghee and panch phoran in a large frying pan over medium heat until the cumin in the panch phoran begins to brown, 2 to 3 minutes. Stir in the onion and salt and cook until the onion is browned around the edges and soft, about 10 minutes. If the onion begins to get too dark or sticks to the bottom of the pan, splash the pan with a bit of water and scrape up the browned bits. Stir in the ground coriander and cook, stirring, for 2 minutes. Stir in the tomatoes and the cayenne and cook until the tomatoes are jammy, 6 to 8 minutes, stirring occasionally. Turn off the heat and set aside.

Once the rice and dal are cooked, remove the lid and use a potato masher to smash the mixture until only a few carrots and peas remain whole (remove the whole or large spices while mashing if you like). Stir in the first tempering oil along with 3 cups/720 ml water. Return to a boil and cook for 2 minutes. Turn off the heat.

To make the second tempering oil: Wipe out the pan from the first tempering oil and heat the ghee for the second tempering oil over medium heat. Add the cumin seeds, cayenne, and asafetida and cook, stirring often, until the cumin begins to brown, about 2 minutes. Immediately stir it into the rice and dal mixture.

Divide the khitcheree among 6 bowls; top with some of the reserved ginger mixture, a pinch of garam masala, and the fried onions; and serve.

TAMARIND CHICKEN WINGS

This is my fallback to offer to company whenever I'm at a loss for what to serve. All you need are chicken wings, which I always have in the freezer, and Tamarind Chutney which I always have canned in the pantry. It never fails to please and is a great way of introducing new flavors like tamarind and Garam Masala in a very friendly, recognizable package (chicken wings!). I have yet to find anyone who regards them as anything less than spectacular. Best yet, the sweet-sour chutney negates the need for a dipping sauce—these wings are excellent on their own. If you must have a dip, I like serving Raita (page 218) on the side made with Greek yogurt for a thicker consistency.

※ ※ ※

Preheat the oven to 400°F/200°C/gas 6. In a small bowl, whisk together the honey, olive oil, salt, cayenne, garam masala, paprika, and cumin. Scrape the mixture into a 1-gl/3.8-L resealable plastic bag, add the chicken wings, turn them to coat in the marinade, and refrigerate for at least 30 minutes or overnight.

Line a rimmed baking sheet with aluminum foil and place a wire cooling rack on top of the baking sheet. Arrange the chicken wings in a single layer on the rack and bake them for 35 minutes.

Remove the wings from the oven and baste them with the chutney. Continue to roast until the wings are slightly charred around the edges and getting crispy, another 15 to 25 minutes. Remove from the oven, sprinkle with salt, and set aside to cool for 5 minutes before serving.

Serves 6

2 tbsp honey

2 tbsp extra-virgin olive oil

1 tsp kosher salt, plus extra for serving

½ tsp cayenne pepper

1 tsp Garam Masala (see page 216)

1 tsp paprika

½ tsp ground cumin

2 lb/910 g chicken wings, halved at the drumette joint

¾ cup/175 ml Tamarind Chutney (page 219)

FARM ✤ YARN

THE BIRDS OF AMERICAN MASALA FARM

When Charlie and I bought our farm, one of our (many) missions was to populate it with heritage breeds of animals from the American Livestock Breeds Conservancy (ALBC) watch list. The ALBC is committed to conserving rare breeds of livestock and ensuring that animals in the United States remain genetically diverse. Not only do the animals add their beauty and charm to the farm, but whenever we host house-guests, we can introduce them to the animals and help others become aware of these uniquely wondrous and endangered creatures that provide both beauty and delicious sustenance.

We started out small, ordering 36 chickens to begin with. Now we have more than 120 and, once a year, we add a few more girls of different breeds—we have more than three dozen varieties of heritage breeds to call our own. Everyone told me that I was crazy for bringing so many breeds

together in the same area, that the chickens would get stressed and not lay eggs. Did we prove them wrong! We get more eggs than we know what to do with. Yes, we do have to protect the prima donnas like the bouffant-coiffed French Crèvecoeurs, Houdans, and Polish girls from the more aggressive girls (in some ways, I wonder if the pretty girls get picked on because the other chickens are jealous), and we have learned to segregate the baby chicks from the grown chickens, but, besides that, there is generally peace and harmony in the henhouse.

Our custom-made coop with its skylights, picture windows that frame pastoral vistas, and high

ceilings (no stooping necessary when it's time to clean the coop or collect eggs) is divided in two, with the smaller part used as the nursery where the chicks stay for about three weeks, without any bullying to contend with, before being allowed to socialize through the chicken fence with the bigger birds. This also gives Charlie and me the opportunity to get to know the new girls, gets them used to being handled and petted, and allows us to spoil them a bit.

Once they are nearly the same size as the more mature girls, they get full access to the coop. We introduce them during the night, because that is when the birds are at their most docile.

You see, the minute the sun sets, chickens pretend that the world has ended—they just drop! We open the coop door, bring the younger birds in, and leave them on a perch. In the morning, they all wake up together and think they have lived together their whole lives. It's a beautiful thing.

The Chickens of American Masala Farm

ANCONA: White-tipped black-feathered birds, once Europe's primary egg-laying breed

ANDALUSIAN: Long-legged blue-toned birds

ARAUCANA: South American birds with incredible copper and metallic-green coloring

BELGIAN D'UCCLE: Beautifully mottled and friendly birds, often referred to as Mille Fleur

BLACK AUSTRALORP: Incredible egg layers with metallic blue-green and black feathers

BROWN-SPOTTED BUTTERCUP: A small ornamental breed from Sicily

BUCKEYE: Friendly birds native to Ohio that are excellent mouse hunters

CHANTECLER: A hardy cold-weather Canadian breed that lays eggs throughout the winter

CUCKOO MARANS: Gentle French hens known for chocolate-brown eggs

DELAWARE: Primarily white-feathered birds that were once the most popular broiler breed in the United States

DOMINIQUE: Developed from the first pilgrim chickens during the settlement of New England

DORKING: One of the oldest breeds of chickens, believed to have been introduced to England by the Romans

FRENCH CRÈVECOEURS: Solid black-crested ornamental birds

HOUDAN: A stunning, speckled, and bearded five-toed and crested chicken related to the Crèvecoeur and Polish breeds.

JERSEY GIANT: The largest pure-breed chickens—hens can weigh up to 10 lb/4.5 kg!

LAKENVELDER: A breed that goes back to the Levant and ancient times

MINORCA: Stately birds with long, angular bodies

NEW HAMPSHIRE RED: Classic red hens that are great egg layers

ORPINGTON: A heavily feathered, hardy English bird

PENEDESENCA: Spanish breed famous for its chocolate-brown-shelled eggs

PHOENIX: A stunning Japanese chicken whose long tail feathers can exceed 20 ft/6 m in length

POLISH: Beautiful breed with large crests of feathers on top of their heads

RHODE ISLAND REDS: Great egg layers

SEBRIGHT: A gorgeous chicken in miniature, with stunning laced plumage

SILVER-SPANGLED HAMBURG: Dalmatian-like speckled birds

WYANDOTTE: An easygoing bird indigenous to New York state

Other Birds at the Farm

Besides our beloved collection of heritage-breed chickens, Charlie and I have amassed flocks of geese, ducks, and even guinea hens.

Contrary to popular belief, heritage geese are not aggressive or mean. Sure, they'll hiss at Charlie and me when we approach them, but once we get close, they clam up and let us take their giant eggs without any fight (just one goose egg is equal to about four chicken eggs). We have mushroom-brown-colored American Buffs and white Tufted Romans, both docile, friendly breeds. They have even crossbred to create Tufted Buffs, adorable geese that look like American Buffs except with a pouf on top of their heads. Although the geese are foragers, we supplement their natural diet with grain. And even though they can't really fly away (they'll only get knee-high off the ground), treating them twice a day to a snack is our way of keeping them comfortable and letting them know that our farm is their home.

The ducks on our farm are from two breeds that need to be preserved: the striking beetle-shell-green Cayuga and the Buff Duck. We bring them in as babies and provide for them during the first few months so that they will think of us as their pack leader. Feeding them grain gets them used to human contact. This way, if we have visitors who want to lift a goose or duck, we can make that happen without a fuss. They forage around but won't leave the farm.

The snappiest birds on the farm are perhaps the most beautiful—the guinea hens. They're so pretty that guests often wonder if they're baby peacocks. While we keep them separate from the chickens (they've killed one of our roosters), they are an important addition to our flock, as they control the ticks on the property. Since we have Lyme disease-causing

deer ticks, we view the guinea hens as a valued addition to our farm. During summertime, they also provide us with delicious eggs just a tad bigger than a quail's. We have many varieties including Jumbo Pearl, Lavender, Buff Dundotte, Slate, Purple, Coral Blue, and Chocolate.

KERALA EGG ROAST

Serves 6

¼ to ⅓ cup/60 to 80 ml canola or grapeseed oil

20 fresh or 30 frozen curry leaves (see page 215)

6 whole cloves

4 bay leaves

4 whole green cardamom pods

2-in/5-cm cinnamon stick

½ tsp cumin seeds

2-in/5-cm piece fresh ginger, peeled and finely minced

4 large red onions, halved and very thinly sliced

½ tsp ground turmeric

1½ tsp kosher salt

¼ tsp fennel seeds

¼ tsp roughly ground black peppercorns

12 hard-boiled eggs, peeled

1 medium tomato, halved, cored, and finely chopped, or ⅓ cup/80 ml canned or boxed chopped tomatoes (preferably the Pomì brand)

1 bunch fresh cilantro, finely chopped

Joshua Thomas, the former executive sous chef at my restaurant, Dévi, stayed with us at the farm one New Year's Eve. It was wonderful ringing in the New Year with a fellow New Yorker, and even better sitting down to the lovely breakfast he made for us on New Year's Day. Joshua made this egg roast, a dish that has been a Christmas Day tradition in his family since he was a child. The key is lots of onions, thinly sliced and slowly cooked until they melt into one another, becoming sticky sweet and deeply flavorful. The eggs are hard-boiled and then cooked in the onions along with tomato and plenty of spices, creating a dish that instantly transported me to the coastal canals of Kerala in southwest India. Charlie and I have made it dozens of times since then, and it never fails to please. Do take the effort to grind the finishing powder in a mortar and pestle just before serving—you will be amply rewarded.

❋ ❋ ❋

Heat the canola oil with the curry leaves, cloves, bay leaves, cardamom, cinnamon stick, and cumin seeds in a large heavy-bottomed pot over medium-high heat until the cinnamon begins to unfurl, 2 to 3 minutes, stirring often so the cumin seeds don't burn. Stir in the ginger and cook until it becomes sticky and fragrant, about 1 minute. Add the onions, turmeric, and salt; reduce the heat to low; and cook, stirring occasionally, until the onions are deeply browned and caramelized, 15 to 20 minutes. If they start to stick to the bottom of the pot or get too dark, splash the pan with a bit of water and stir up the sticky bits at the bottom of the pot.

While the onions caramelize, grind the fennel seeds and peppercorns into a fine powder using a mortar and pestle or spice grinder (if using a spice grinder, you may need to double the amount so that the spices get finely ground).

Add the hard-boiled eggs to the pan with the onions and gently roll them to coat with the onion mixture. Fry the eggs until a light brown skin forms, 2 to 3 minutes. Stir the tomato into the pot and cook, stirring occasionally, until the tomato juices have evaporated and the onions look jammy, 4 to 6 minutes. Stir in the cilantro, cook for 1 minute, and then stir in the fennel-peppercorn powder. Serve immediately.

VEAL CHOPS WITH
MUSTARD-HERB SAUCE

When it comes to entertaining, Charlie and I are not known for our restraint, and there are a few dishes we have created that get requested time and time again by friends who visit. This is one of those dishes, first served to our dear friends from England. They couldn't stop talking about it, so we decided to try it out on others and, before we knew it, these simple pan-seared chops with an aromatic mustard sauce became one of our most-requested dinner recipes. It is made extra-special by the beautiful long-bone veal chops from Allen Brothers, a specialty meat purveyor known for its sinfully delicious beef, lamb, and humanely raised Meadow Reserve veal. The meat is so succulent, tender, and melt-in-your-mouth incredible that we try to fuss with it as little as possible. While adding bacon and crème fraîche may seem like gilding the lily, they'll elicit outrageous groans of pleasure from your tablemates and are well worth the splurge. I serve this with the Farmhouse Crispy-Creamy Potatoes on page 43 and some-times a simple roasted vegetable.

❋ ❋ ❋

Season both sides of the chops liberally with salt and pepper and set aside.

Heat the canola oil in a large frying pan over medium heat. Add the bacon and fry until lightly browned, stirring occasionally, 3 to 5 minutes. Use a slotted spoon to transfer the bacon to a small bowl and set aside.

Add the onions to the frying pan and cook, stirring often, until they're evenly browned on all sides, 7 to 10 minutes. Use a slotted spoon to transfer them to a medium bowl and set aside.

Increase the heat to medium-high, place the chops in the frying pan, and cook without moving until they're nicely seared and brown, 3 to 4 min-utes. Use a spatula to flip the chops and sear the other side, 2 to 3 minutes longer. Transfer the chops to a large plate and set aside.

continued . . .

Serves 4

Four 8-oz/225-g veal chops

Kosher salt

Freshly ground black pepper

1 tbsp canola or grapeseed oil

8 strips bacon, sliced crosswise into ¼-in/6-mm pieces

24 pearl onions, peeled, or 2 large red onions, coarsely chopped

½ tsp finely minced fresh rosemary

½ tsp finely minced fresh thyme

¼ tsp finely minced fresh lemon verbena (optional)

1 tbsp all-purpose flour

¾ cup/175 ml rich white wine (like an un-oaky Chardonnay)

¾ cup/175 ml room-temperature veal or beef stock, plus ⅓ cup/ 80 ml if necessary

⅓ cup/80 ml crème fraîche, store-bought or homemade (page 214), or ⅓ cup/80 ml heavy cream

2 tbsp Dijon mustard

1 tbsp finely chopped fresh flat-leaf parsley

Stir the rosemary, thyme, lemon verbena (if using), and ¼ tsp pepper into the drippings in the pan and cook until they become fragrant, 1 to 2 minutes. While stirring constantly, stir in the flour and cook for 1 minute before whisking in the wine, making sure to completely incorporate it into the flour mixture before pouring in the stock. Bring to a boil and then return the bacon and chops to the pan, making sure the chops are resting flat on the bottom of the frying pan. Return the onions to the frying pan, cover, reduce the heat to low, and cook until the chops are just slightly underdone (they'll be soft in the center), about 25 minutes. Uncover the frying pan, turn the chops over, re-cover, and cook until the chops are cooked to your liking, 5 to 8 minutes for medium-rare or 8 to 10 minutes for medium. (At this point, if the sauce seems jammy rather than saucy, add up to ⅓ cup/80 ml more stock.)

Transfer the chops to individual plates or a serving platter and stir the crème fraîche into the sauce. Bring to a simmer, then stir in the mustard and parsley. Turn off the heat immediately (if allowed to simmer, the sauce will become bitter). Adjust the sauce with salt and pepper if needed, spoon it over the chops, and serve.

MASALA CHATEAUBRIAND

Serves 6

One 2-lb/910-g beef tenderloin roast (preferably Wagyu beef)

3 tbsp extra-virgin olive oil

3 garlic cloves, pressed through a garlic press or finely minced

¼ cup/15 g chopped mixed fresh herbs (basil, oregano, rosemary, thyme), or 2 tbsp dried mixed herbs (Herbes de Hebron, page 215, or herbes de Provence are nice)

1 tbsp kosher salt

1 tbsp freshly ground black or mixed peppercorns

2 garlic cloves, each cut lengthwise into 4 strips

For holidays and special gatherings, few cuts can surpass a chateaubriand beef tenderloin. Without any bones to navigate, it's easy to carve at the table, and its tenderness and juicy qualities make it a crowd favorite. Nothing proves that fact more than praise from your guests. One Christmas Eve at the farm, our caretaker, Mark Durrin, and his fifteen-year-old son, Austin, joined us at the table. After Austin's third helping of the chateaubriand, he said that if this was the quality of the meat we always served at our table, he'd be happy to join us for a meal anytime. If a young adult can be so effusive about quality, that's all the encouragement I need to justify the expense and the splurge. Since the meat is so lovely, I keep the preparation simple—just some spices and herbs—that's it. One guest said that the simplicity and ease alone justify the cost of the roast, while another contended that eating a quality steak at home far surpasses any pricey steakhouse experience. When the steak is served alongside our Farmhouse Crispy-Creamy Potatoes (page 43), Simple Marinated Peppers (page 86), cranberry relish, coleslaw, and cornbread, I'd have to agree. Wagyu beef tenderloin (the beautifully marbled beef that made Kobe, Japan, famous) from Allen Brothers is a total splurge, but well worth it, especially when you're gathered with special friends and family during the holidays. It's easy to cook more than one roast for more guests, too.

❁ ❁ ❁

Remove the meat from the refrigerator and place it on a rimmed baking sheet. Let it sit out for 1 hour (bringing the meat up to room temperature will help it to cook more evenly).

In a small bowl, whisk together the olive oil, minced garlic, and herbs and rub the mixture all over the roast. Then rub the roast with the salt and pepper. Using a paring knife, make eight small ¾-in-/2-cm-deep slits all over the roast and insert a garlic strip into each slit. Set the roast aside for 1 hour longer.

Preheat the oven to 450°F/230°C/gas 8. Place the roast in a roasting pan and cook for 10 minutes. Reduce the oven temperature to 350°F/180°C/gas 4 and bake for another 15 to 25 minutes, depending on how you like your meat cooked. Insert an instant-read thermometer into the center of the roast to check its internal temperature, pulling the roast out from the oven when it's 10°F/6°C shy of your preferred temperature range—125°F to 130°F/51°C to 54°C for rare, 130°F to 135°F/54°C to 57°C for medium-rare, 135°F to 140°F/57°C to 60°C for medium. (The meat on the ends of the roast are often more well done than the meat in the center of the roast.) Remove the roast from the oven, loosely tent with aluminum foil, and set aside for 10 minutes to rest. Carve and serve on a platter.

VARIATION: GILDED LILY WHISKEY GRAVY

After removing the roast from the roasting pan, place the roasting pan over medium-high heat. Stir in ½ tsp freshly ground black pepper, cook for 1 minute, and then deglaze the pan with ¼ cup/60 ml whiskey (we love Suntory Hibiki 12-year-old whiskey), being sure to scrape up any browned bits off the bottom of the roasting pan. Whisk in ½ cup/115 g crème fraîche, turn off the heat, adjust the flavor with salt and pepper, and serve alongside the roast.

CANDY CANE KISSES

These are a must at our house during the holidays. The only problem is that they never last—I have been known to eat a dozen within minutes! The recipe comes from a pastry chef friend, Allison Heaton, who grew up in Austin, Texas, and learned how to make these from her dad, Kencil Heaton. A retired Air National Guard general, he was raised eating these airy, sweet, and minty meringues. Though Allison now makes them with fancy 75 to 85 percent cacao bittersweet chocolate bars, she learned to make them with semisweet chocolate chips courtesy of air force ration supplies. So feel free to use what you prefer. When candy canes fall out of favor at the farm (anytime before December 1 and after January 1), I substitute 1 teaspoon finely pulverized dried lavender (you can grind lavender in a spice grinder or use a mortar and pestle).

Makes 4½ dozen cookies

4 egg whites, at room temperature

¼ tsp cream of tartar

⅛ tsp fine salt

1½ cups/300 g sugar

3 tbsp crushed candy canes

8 oz/225 g semisweet chocolate, finely chopped

1 tsp vanilla extract

A few drops of red food coloring (optional)

❋ ❋ ❋

Heat the oven to 250°F/120°C/gas ½. Line three rimmed baking sheets with parchment paper and set aside. (If you don't have three baking sheets, be sure to allow the baking sheet to cool completely before baking the second and third batches of meringues.)

Using a stand mixer or a hand mixer, beat the egg whites on medium speed until they're foamy. Add the cream of tartar and salt, increase the speed to medium-high, and beat until soft peaks form. With the mixer running, add the sugar, 1 tbsp at a time, and beat until the whites are glossy and hold stiff peaks. Remove the bowl from the mixer and add the crushed candy canes, chocolate, vanilla, and food coloring (if using). Use a rubber spatula to fold the ingredients into the meringue.

Measure out 1-tbsp dollops of meringue onto the prepared baking sheets. Bake the meringues until they begin to crack on top, 45 to 50 minutes. Remove from the oven and let them cool completely on wire racks. Store the cookies for up to 5 days in an airtight container at room temperature.

CRANBERRY AND DRIED STRAWBERRY FREE-FORM GALETTE

Serves 6

1 tart dough (see Rustic Double Apple Tart, page 153)

¼ cup/35 g almonds

¼ cup/30 g panko bread crumbs

3 cups/300 g fresh or thawed frozen cranberries (if using frozen, thaw them on paper towels)

1 apple, peeled, cored, and cut into ¼- to ½-in/6- to 12-mm pieces

¼ cup/30 g dried strawberries, roughly chopped

¼ cup/60 g strawberry jam, either store-bought or homemade (see page 109)

1 cup/200 g packed light brown sugar

Zest of 1 lemon

2-in/5-cm piece ginger, peeled and finely minced

⅛ tsp ground ginger

⅛ tsp ground cardamom

1 large egg

1½ tbsp granulated sugar

Confectioners' sugar for serving

We moved to the farm from Manhattan just two months before the holidays. Charlie and I concluded that the best way to get to know our neighbors was to host a New Year's Eve party and make all of our favorite foods, like New Year's Black-Eyed Pea Curry (page 184), Shortcut Potato and Pea Turnovers (page 178), and a massive selection of desserts for guests to nibble on well into the midnight hour. While we expected around twenty guests, we ended up with sixty! So for our second New Year's Eve bash, I planned for about eighty revelers (more than ninety showed up) and cooked for the feast all week long. I made dozens of dishes in the days leading up to the party and, by December 30, had only enough galette dough for one last tart. With one bag of fresh cranberries and a pantry full of dried fruits, I came up with this delightful sweet-sour and rustic galette that has since become a much-requested favorite dessert—even in the summertime when I have to count on frozen cranberries to make it. A simple and sure-bet crowd-pleaser, I made this for a Slow Food Saratoga fund-raiser and the chapter founder, John Sconzo, and his son, Michael, saw the tart, grabbed it, and sequestered themselves off in a corner where they (along with a few select friends) happily devoured it without sharing. Easy to make and light on the fuss, this galette always pleases big-time.

❊ ❊ ❊

Preheat the oven to 375°F/190°C/gas 5. Place the dough between two 15-in-/38-cm-long pieces of parchment paper and roll into a 13- to 14-in-/33- to 35.5-cm-wide and ⅛-in-/3-mm-thick circle. Peel off the top layer of parchment, lift the bottom piece of parchment (and the dough), and place it on a rimmed baking sheet. Place the sheet in the refrigerator.

Use a food processor to coarsely grind the almonds so some are fine like a powder and others are rough textured like bread crumbs. Place the almonds in a small bowl and stir in the panko.

In a medium bowl, use your hands to toss together the cranberries, apple, strawberries, jam, brown sugar, minced ginger, lemon zest, ground ginger, and cardamom. Set aside.

Remove the baking sheet from the refrigerator. Place the almond-panko mixture in the center of the dough and use your hands to spread it into a 9-in/23-cm circle. Spoon the cranberry filling over the crumbs. Fold the edges of the dough over the filling, overlapping them as you go, so there is about a 4-in/10-cm circle of filling in the center of the galette.

Whisk the egg in a small bowl and brush it over the pastry. Sprinkle the pastry with the granulated sugar and bake it until the filling is bubbly and the crust is golden, 30 to 40 minutes. Remove the baking sheet from the oven and let the tart cool for at least 10 minutes before using a spatula to gently separate it from the parchment and transfer it to a platter. Serve hot, warm, or at room temperature dusted with confectioners' sugar.

CHOCOLATE-NUT BRITTLE

**Makes one 11-by-17-in/
28-by-43-cm pan**

FOR THE CHOCOLATE

11 oz/310 g chocolate (60 to
72 percent cacao), finely chopped

¼ tsp ground cardamom

¼ tsp ground ginger

¼ tsp ground mace

⅛ tsp ground allspice

Scant ⅛ tsp ground cloves

Scant ⅛ tsp cayenne pepper
(optional)

FOR THE BRITTLE

2 lb/910 g good-quality salted
butter, cut into chunks, plus 1 tbsp
at room temperature

4½ cups/620 g chopped and toasted
nuts (I like a combination of peanuts
and slivered almonds)

¼ tsp ground cardamom

¼ tsp ground ginger

3 cups/600 g sugar

⅓ cup/80 ml water

2 tbsp light corn syrup

1 tsp fresh lemon juice

*I feel confident in saying that this is the best toffee-nut brittle you will
ever eat. Of course, it depends on using high-quality chocolate, that's more
semisweet than bittersweet, and good salted butter—my favorite is golden
yellow Kerrygold from Ireland (available in many supermarkets). A beautiful antique tin lined with parchment paper or wax paper and packed
with homemade brittle makes a wonderful holiday gift. You can even freeze
it and break it out for an easy afternoon sweet alongside a cup of steaming
Farmhouse Chai (page 168). If you're into sweet-salty confections, you'll
love this with roasted and salted peanuts instead of plain toasted nuts. I
am partial to the soft heat that a pinch of cayenne lends to the brittle, but
it can be left out for a more traditional taste.*

❋ ❋ ❋

To make the chocolate: Place the chocolate, cardamom, ginger, mace,
allspice, cloves, and cayenne (if using) in a medium bowl. Bring 2 in/
5 cm of water to a simmer in a medium saucepan. Reduce the heat to
low, place the bowl with the chocolate and spices over the hot water, and
let it sit there, stirring every 1 to 2 minutes, until the chocolate is melted,
4 to 6 minutes.

To make the brittle: Lightly grease the bottom and sides of an 11-by-17-in/
28-by-43-cm rimmed baking sheet with 1 tbsp room-temperature butter.
Fit the baking sheet with a piece of parchment paper, press it down to
grease the underside, and then turn the parchment paper over so that
the buttered side is up.

Place 3 cups/415 g of the toasted nuts, the cardamom, and ginger in a
large bowl and stir to combine. Set aside.

Melt the remaining 2 lb/910 g butter in a large saucepan over medium-
high heat. Stir in the sugar, water, corn syrup, and lemon juice and
bring the mixture to a boil, stirring occasionally to ensure that the sugar
is completely melted. Once the mixture comes to a boil, stop stirring.
Using a pastry brush, dab the sides of the pot with water if you see sugar
crystallizing. Continue to cook the caramel until it reads 300°F/150°C
on an instant-read thermometer, 25 to 30 minutes, swirling the pan

continued . . .

occasionally to ensure that the caramel cooks evenly. (If the caramel starts to bubble and rise to the lip of the saucepan, reduce the heat.) Turn off the heat, stir in the spiced nuts (be careful not to spatter the piping-hot sugar), and immediately pour the mixture onto the greased baking sheet. Set the pan aside for 4 minutes and then pour the melted chocolate over the brittle, using an offset spatula to spread the chocolate in an even layer. Sprinkle the remaining 1½ cups/205 g nuts over the chocolate and set aside to cool completely, either overnight at room temperature or covered with plastic wrap and in the refrigerator, for at least 3 hours.

Break the brittle into irregular pieces and serve on a platter or store them in an airtight container or in a 1-gl/3.8-L freezer bag for up to 3 months.

CHOCOLATE-PEANUT TART
WITH CARAMEL AND
CHOCOLATE MOUSSE

This tart is a love affair between chocolate and peanuts. Like many not born in America, I don't share the national love of peanut butter (though I do love to cook with and eat peanuts), but in this tart I accept peanut butter for all of its creamy, salty, nutty glory! Frank Vollkommer (a Certified Master Pastry Chef—there are only thirteen such chefs in the world!) is responsible for this sweet, salty, caramely, peanuty, überchocolate creation, and works his thrilling magic with anything chocolate-related at The Chocolate Mill in Glens Falls, not far from the farm. When he and his wife, Jessica, opened the shop, I confess that I was nervous for them, worried that such talent could not be sustained by our local economy and taste buds. Luckily, their tempting creations speak for themselves, and they are successful and thriving. Butter toffee peanuts from Royal Oak really send this tart over the top, but simple toasted peanuts are perfectly wonderful, too. Making this tart requires time and patience on the part of the cook—so I double my efforts and make two, freezing one for another time. The tart dough is very delicate—be sure to use lots of flour when you roll it out (and brush away excess flour using a pastry brush before transferring the dough to the tart pan tin with removable bottom).

❋ ❋ ❋

To make the crust: Whisk together the pastry flour, peanut flour, cocoa, and salt in a medium bowl and set aside.

In the bowl of a stand mixer (or large bowl if using a hand mixer), cream together the butter and sugar on medium-high speed until the mixture is pale and aerated, about 2 minutes. Whisk together the egg, egg yolk, milk, and vanilla in a liquid measuring cup and add the mixture to the creamed butter and egg mixture a little at a time until it's completely incorporated, scraping the bottom and sides of the bowl as necessary.

continued . . .

Makes two 8-in/20-cm tarts

FOR THE CRUST

2¼ cups/255 g pastry flour, plus extra for rolling

⅔ cup/80 g peanut flour

2½ tbsp Dutch-processed cocoa powder

¼ tsp fine salt

11 tbsp/310 g unsalted butter, at room temperature

½ cup/100 g sugar

1 egg, plus 1 egg yolk

1½ tsp milk

1 tsp vanilla extract

FOR THE CARAMEL

1¼ cups/250 g sugar

⅓ cup/80 ml water

6 tbsp/90 ml heavy cream

12 tbsp/340 g unsalted butter

½ tsp vanilla bean paste or scraped seeds from ½ vanilla bean

¼ tsp fine salt

continued . . .

FOR THE CHOCOLATE MOUSSE

1⅓ cups/320 ml heavy cream

2 eggs, plus 1 egg yolk

¼ cup/50 g plus 1 tbsp sugar

3 tbsp cold water

2½ tsp gelatin

6 oz/170 g semisweet chocolate (60 to 72 percent cacao), melted

FOR FINISHING THE TARTS

6 oz/170 g semisweet chocolate (60 to 72 percent cacao), melted

Scant 1 cup/225 g smooth peanut butter

¾ cup/110 g finely chopped roasted peanuts

¾ cup/110 g roughly chopped Royal Oak Butter Toffee Peanuts (or crushed roasted peanuts)

Add the dry ingredients and mix on low speed until the dough comes together in a ball. Divide the dough in half, shape each into a flat disc (about ½ in/12 mm thick) and wrap in plastic wrap. Refrigerate for at least 1 hour or up to 2 days before rolling.

Remove the dough from the refrigerator and unwrap it. Lightly flour your worksurface and roll each piece of dough into a ¼-in-/6-mm-thick circle. Line two 8-in/20-cm tart pans with removable bottoms with the dough, pushing the dough into the sides of the pans, and pinching off the top. Chill for 30 minutes.

Heat the oven to 350°F/180°C/gas 4. Line the pans with parchment paper and place dried beans or pie weights in each shell. Place the pans on a rimmed baking sheet and bake for 15 minutes. Remove the pans from the oven and gently lift out the parchment (with the beans or pie weights). Return the crusts to the oven, and bake until dry and set, 10 to 15 minutes longer. Set the crusts aside to cool completely.

To make the caramel: Place the sugar and water in a medium heavy-bottomed saucepan and gently stir over medium heat until the sugar dissolves. Increase the heat to medium-high and cook until the liquid turns a deep brown amber color, swirling the mixture occasionally (by holding the saucepan by the handle, not by stirring), about 12 minutes (occasionally brush the sides of the saucepan with a pastry brush dipped in water if you see crystallization on the sides of the pan). Remove from the heat, pour in the cream, and then whisk in the butter, vanilla, and salt. Set aside.

To make the mousse: Use a stand mixer or a large bowl and a hand mixer to whip the cream to medium peaks. Cover the bowl with plastic wrap and refrigerate. Bring 1 in/2.5 cm water to a simmer in a medium saucepan. Place the eggs, egg yolk, and sugar in a large metal bowl and set the bowl over the simmering water. Reduce the heat to low and whip the eggs and sugar until the mixture is very pale yellow, thick, and ribbons when the whisk is lifted out from the mixture.

Pour the cold water into a small bowl or ramekin, and sprinkle the gelatin over the top. Set aside for 5 minutes to bloom and then whisk it into the whipped egg and sugar mixture. Whisk in the chocolate and whisk vigorously to combine. Remove the whipped cream from the refrigerator and fold it into the chocolate mixture. Scrape the mousse into a large bowl, cover with plastic wrap, and refrigerate.

To finish the tarts: Place the cooled tart shells on your worksurface. Brush the bottom and sides of the tart shells with the melted chocolate. Scrape the peanut butter into a pastry bag fitted with a small round tip and pipe the peanut butter around the edge of each tart crust (where the sides meet the bottom). Pipe another circle around the center of the tart shell bottom. Sprinkle half of the roasted peanuts into the bottom of the tarts. Divide the caramel between the bottom of the two tarts (if it is too hard, warm it slightly so it's pourable), sprinkle the remaining roasted peanuts over the caramel, and chill the crusts for about 20 minutes to set the caramel.

Remove the mousse from the refrigerator and whisk it to soften so it can be piped. Fill another clean pastry bag fitted with a round tip with the chocolate mousse and pipe small dots on top of each tart so that the filling beneath the mousse doesn't show at all. Sprinkle the butter toffee peanuts between the two tarts and chill until serving.

If you plan to freeze one tart, once the tart has chilled, wrap it in several layers of plastic wrap and place it in a resealable 1-gl/3.8-L freezer bag (you may need to use more than one bag to completely enclose the tart). Freeze for up to 2 weeks and thaw in the refrigerator overnight before serving.

FARMHOUSE BASICS

These are the ingredients and basic recipes that are in constant play in our kitchen. I call for them throughout the book and find them indispensable.

Asafetida

Pungent asafetida smells like a cross between onion and garlic and comes from the root of a plant. Ground into a powder, it is used in minuscule amounts to flavor food almost as you might use garlic or onion powder. It is available at Indian markets and online (see Farmhouse Resources, page 222). If you don't have any on hand, don't let it stop you from making a recipe—just omit it.

Chaat Masala

This is one of my absolute favorite spice blends. *Chaat* masala commonly includes spices like cayenne, cumin, coriander, garam masala, ginger, ground fennel, carom seed (*ajwain*), asafetida, paprika, dried mint, black pepper, and black salt (*sanchal*) among other spices. In Hindi, the word *chaat* literally means "to lick," referring to *chaat* masala's combination of spices that absolutely induces salivation. It is most commonly sprinkled over small dishes of crunchy, cooling snacks called *chaat*—a few classics are *papri chaat*, an amazing combination of crunchy lentil wafers, chickpeas, sweet-sour tamarind chutney, boiled potatoes, tangy plain yogurt, and *bhel puri*. *Chaat* masala is wonderful sprinkled over grilled corn and finished with a squeeze of lime juice, or sprinkled over sweet-potato fries. It's available in Indian markets or online (see Farmhouse Resources, page 222).

Cheese

We always have on hand a large selection of locally made artisanal cheeses for snacking, cheese boards, and cooking (see Farmhouse Resources, page 222, for North Country cheesemakers). From hard cave-aged cheese to fresh cheese, brined cheese to soft-rind cheese, we love it all, especially the crottins, wedges, and logs crafted by our beloved cheesemaker friends and neighbors. Feel free to substitute any like-minded artisanal cheese for any quantities called for in the book. For example, we might use Consider Bardwell Farm's Manchester goat cheese instead of the aged cheddar in the Summer Tomato Pie (page 88) or sheep's milk ricotta instead of chèvre in the Goat Cheese and Herb Frittata (page 30).

Crème Fraîche

There is nothing like the silky texture and tang of homemade crème fraîche. Making it is quite simple—Charlie likes starting with a little bit of leftover crème fraîche from the last batch if he has it. If not, he starts fresh following this recipe.

3 cups/720 ml heavy cream

I cup/240 ml buttermilk

Juice of I lemon (optional)

Place the cream, buttermilk, and lemon juice (if using) in a medium saucepan over low heat and heat until the mixture has lost its chill and is warm to the touch (do not microwave the liquid). Pour it into a glass bowl, cover with a clean kitchen towel, and then place a plate on top of the towel. Set aside in a warm (approximately 70°F/20°C) spot for 24 hours. Remove the plate and kitchen towel, whisk the crème fraîche, cover with plastic wrap, and refrigerate for up to 2 weeks. Makes about 4 cups/960 ml.

Curry Leaves

Curry leaves, which look like small, shiny bay laurel, have a citrusy flavor that unfortunately has no substitute. You can almost always find them in Indian markets and even sometimes in natural foods stores. Buy them in bulk and freeze them to use later—they'll stay fresh for 4 to 6 months frozen. If using frozen curry leaves, use about 1½ times the quantity of fresh.

Dried Red Chiles

I use a lot of whole chiles in my food—more to add warmth than spice (it's the seeds that add spice—keeping chiles whole keeps the lid on the heat). You can always reduce the quantity of chiles called for in a recipe to what your preference is.

Herbed Chèvre

Cheese is a seasonal product, and Charlie refuses to let the last beautiful crottins of fresh chèvre slip past us without preserving several rounds to get us through autumn and the first few weeks of winter.

2 cups/480 ml good-quality extra-virgin olive oil

A few sprigs each of fresh oregano, thyme, and winter savory

1 sprig fresh rosemary

3 dried red chiles

2 bay leaves

1 tbsp whole mixed peppercorns

Three to four 8-oz/225-g rounds fresh goat's milk chèvre

Pour the olive oil into a medium saucepan. Add the fresh herbs, chiles, bay leaves, and peppercorns and warm over medium heat until the mixture comes to a simmer. Simmer until fragrant, 1 minute, turn off the heat, and set aside to cool completely.

Place one crottin of cheese into a large sterilized jar (see page 159 for information about how to sterilize jars) and cover with some of the cooled herb-infused oil. Repeat with each crottin and more oil, ending with the remaining oil, herbs, and spices. Seal the jar, date it, and store in a cool, dark place to cure for at least 1 month before opening. The cheese can remain preserved for up to 3 months. Makes 3 or 4 rounds of herbed chèvre.

Herbes de Hebron

Our herb garden flanks the side entrance to the house, greeting guests even before Charlie or I do. We couldn't stop ourselves from planting all kinds of lovely herbs, from simple chives and mint to more exotic lemon verbena and lavender. Throughout the summer and into the fall, we collect the fresh herbs and bundle them, then hang them to dry from a peg in the entryway. Using your own dried herbs will elevate the flavor of your food beyond what you could ever hope for. This is my take on herbes de Provence, a blend of flavors used in the French countryside on everything from chicken to lamb and in soups and salads. For a finer texture, you can pulse the blend once or twice in a small food processor, spice grinder, or, if you have patience and resilience, a mortar and pestle.

1 tbsp dried basil

1 tbsp dried lavender

1 tbsp dried oregano

1 tbsp dried rosemary

1 tbsp dried thyme

1 tsp dried chives

1 tsp dried summer savory

¾ tsp freshly ground black pepper

Place the herbs in a small bowl and mix to combine. Store in an airtight container in a cool, dry, and dark spot for up to 6 months. Makes about ⅓ cup/20 g.

Garam Masala

Garam masala is perhaps the most well-known Indian spice blend (aside from curry powder—more on that on page 187). It's a northern spice, used in places like New Delhi and the Northern Plains, where the winters are harsh. The spices used in this mix—cinnamon, cloves, and chiles—have a warming effect, making the addition of garam masala to recipes not just delicious but useful too.

1-in/2.5-cm cinnamon stick, broken into pieces

4 bay leaves

¼ cup/4 g cumin seeds

⅓ cup/6 g coriander seeds

6 whole green cardamom pods

2 whole brown cardamom pods

1 tbsp whole black peppercorns

1 tbsp whole cloves

1 dried red chile

¼ tsp freshly grated nutmeg

⅛ tsp ground mace

Heat the cinnamon, bay leaves, cumin seeds, coriander seeds, cardamom, peppercorns, cloves, and chile in a medium frying pan over medium-high heat, stirring often, until the cumin becomes brown, 2½ to 3 minutes.

Transfer the spices to a baking sheet to cool. Once cooled, transfer the spices to a spice grinder, coffee mill, or small food processor, add the nutmeg and mace, and grind to a fine powder. Store in an airtight container for up to 4 months.

Ghee (Clarified Butter)

Ghee is the clarified butter of India made by melting butter, letting the milk solids settle to the bottom of the pan, and then spooning off the golden liquid, leaving the milky whey behind. Ghee is quite expensive, and in India food is often cooked in oil instead and then ghee is stirred in at the end, used almost like a spice to flavor the dish. Because of its long cooking process, ghee doesn't need to be refrigerated and can be stored in a moisture-free, dark, and cool environment after opening. To make your own clarified butter, simply melt butter in a pot, turn off the heat, let the milk solids settle, and then spoon the yellow melted butter off the top.

Green Chutney

There are a few homemade chutneys that I am never without—*haree* chutney is one of them (tamarind chutney and tomato chutney are two others—see pages 219 and 221 for the recipes). It's amazing with anything and everything, giving even the most simple dish a beautiful, fresh, and incredibly bright flavor. In the summer, I'll add ¾ cup/180 ml plain yogurt for a refreshing creamy chutney.

1½ cups/25 g firmly packed fresh cilantro

½ cup/8 g firmly packed fresh mint leaves

4 scallions, white and light green parts only

2 or 3 fresh green chiles (like jalapeños or serranos), stemmed and roughly chopped (seeded for less heat)

2-in/5-cm piece ginger, peeled and roughly chopped

Juice of 2 lemons

1 tbsp sugar

½ tsp salt

¼ cup/60 ml water

Place the cilantro, mint, scallions, chiles, ginger, lemon juice, sugar, salt, and water in a blender and purée (it doesn't purée smoothly—you'll have to stop and scrape down the sides and bottom of the blender jar often) until completely smooth. Transfer to an airtight container and refrigerate for up to 3 days. Makes 1½ cups/355 ml.

Mayonnaise

Homemade mayonnaise is an entirely different species when compared to store-bought mayo. Creamy, rich, and wonderful, it's dangerously delicious!

1 egg yolk, at room temperature

2 tsp Dijon mustard, at room temperature

⅔ cup/160 ml canola or grapeseed oil

⅓ cup/80 ml extra-virgin olive oil

1 tbsp honey

2 tsp Champagne vinegar

1 tsp Boyajian lemon oil

½ tsp freshly ground pepper (preferably mixed peppercorns, but black pepper is fine)

Kosher salt

Place the egg yolk and mustard in a medium bowl and whisk to combine. Pour the canola oil and olive oil into a large measuring cup and drizzle them in, a small amount at a time, while whisking constantly, to create an emulsion. As the mixture gets thick, creamy, and more voluminous, you can add a little more oil at a time until all of the oil is added. Whisk in the honey, vinegar, lemon oil, and pepper. Season with salt, cover with plastic wrap (or transfer to an airtight container), and chill until serving. The mayonnaise keeps in the refrigerator for up to 3 days. Makes about 1¼ cups/300 ml.

Oil

I keep several types of oils in my kitchen: good-quality extra-virgin olive oil, of course, lovely for roasting and finishing; neutral-flavored oil for blooming spices and pan-frying—I like canola oil, grapeseed oil (which also has a high burn point, making it useful for deep frying), and vegetable oil; peanut oil is my oil of choice for deep frying. Its high smoke point makes for the crispest, cleanest-tasting fries.

Panch Phoran

This is a whole-spice blend that is similar to garam masala, except that *panch phoran* adds texture as well as flavor. While it is most often used whole, *panch phoran* can be pulverized in a spice grinder or by using a mortar and pestle and added to curries like the Shrimp and Sweet Corn Curry on page 97.

I tbsp cumin seeds

I tbsp fennel seeds

I tbsp brown mustard seeds

I tbsp nigella seeds

I tbsp fenugreek seeds

Mix together and store in an airtight container for up to 1 year. Makes 5 tbsp/25 g.

Raita

Simple, soothing, healthful, and delicious, this is a staple at our home.

1¼ tsp cumin seeds

I tsp coriander seeds

½ tsp whole black peppercorns

2½ cups/600 ml plain yogurt

I small cucumber, peeled and finely chopped

I small red onion, finely chopped

I small tomato, finely chopped

2 fresh green chiles (like jalapeños or serranos), very finely chopped (optional)

I tsp finely chopped fresh mint, or ¼ tsp dried mint

¼ tsp cayenne pepper

¼ tsp kosher salt

¼ cup/10 g finely chopped fresh cilantro

Place the cumin seeds, coriander seeds, and peppercorns in a small frying pan over medium heat and toast, shaking the pan often, until they're fragrant and the cumin is golden brown, about 2 minutes. Transfer the spices to a small plate to cool and then grind them using a spice grinder or coffee mill.

Whisk the yogurt in a large bowl until it's smooth. Stir in the cucumber, onion, tomato, chiles (if using), and mint. Stir in the toasted spices and the cayenne. If serving immediately, stir in the salt and finish with the cilantro. Or cover with plastic wrap and refrigerate, stirring in the salt and cilantro just before serving. Makes about 3 cups/710 ml.

Salt

I use kosher salt or sea salt for cooking, fine salt for baking, and flaky sea salt (like Maldon) for finishing. According to my good friend Amy Myrdal Miller, the program director of strategic initiatives at the Culinary Institute of America, we perceive things as saltier when there is salt on the surface of the food rather than baked into it. The example she likes to use is potato chips versus crackers. Crackers are perceived to be much less salty than potato chips, but, in fact, chips often have less salt than crackers! That's why I like to use kosher salt in cooking (it's coarser than table salt and it is easy to control the amount when sprinkled into food) and finish with a sprinkle of sea salt (which has slightly less sodium chloride than table and kosher salts). If I'm cooking for someone with health issues who has to watch his/her salt intake, I know I can reduce the amount of salt in the process of cooking and season the food just before serving. The difference in taste is only slightly detectable, but the difference in your health can be exponential.

Sambhaar Powder

The southern Indian equivalent to garam masala, this blend tastes the most like what Americans and those across the pond might call "curry powder." I hold back on the amount of pungent fenugreek, but for a stronger and more traditional flavor, double it.

3 dried red chiles

2 tbsp coriander seeds

2 tbsp brown mustard seeds

1 tbsp cumin seeds

2 tsp fenugreek seeds

1 tbsp urad dal (white lentils)

1 tbsp channa dal (yellow lentils)

2 tsp roughly ground black pepper

40 fresh curry leaves (see page 215; optional—only use fresh curry leaves, not frozen)

Place the chiles, coriander seeds, mustard seeds, cumin seeds, fenugreek seeds, urad dal, channa dal, pepper, and curry leaves (if using) in a medium frying pan over medium-high heat and toast, shaking the frying pan often, until the mustard seeds begin to pop, 3½ to 5 minutes. Transfer to a large plate to cool and then grind in a coffee mill or spice grinder. Store in an airtight container for up to 4 months. Makes about ¾ cup/60 g.

Tamarind Chutney

Sweet, sour, and addictive, tamarind chutney is like the barbecue sauce of India. I make it using tamarind concentrate, which lasts for ages in the refrigerator. It's available at ethnic markets and online (see Farmhouse Resources, page 222). This chutney can be refrigerated for up to 2 weeks—not that it will last that long.

1 tbsp canola or grapeseed oil

1 tsp ground ginger

1 tsp cumin seeds

½ tsp fennel seeds

½ tsp cayenne pepper

½ tsp asafetida (see page 214; optional)

½ tsp Garam Masala (page 216)

2 cups/240 ml water

1¼ cups/250 g sugar

3 tbsp tamarind concentrate

Heat the canola oil, ginger, cumin seeds, fennel seeds, cayenne, asafetida (if using), and garam masala in a medium saucepan over medium-high heat until the cumin is fragrant and lightly toasted, shaking the pan often, about 1 minute. Whisk in the water, sugar, and tamarind concentrate until it is completely dissolved. Bring to a boil, reduce the heat to medium, and simmer until the sauce turns dark brown and is thick enough to leave a trail on the back of a wooden spoon, 20 to 30 minutes. Turn off the heat and set aside (it will thicken as it cools). Makes about 1 cup/300 ml.

Toasted Cumin

Keep a small container of toasted cumin in your spice cabinet at all times. It adds a beautiful nuttiness to everything from vegetables to chili, guacamole, and spice rubs.

½ cup/8 g cumin seeds

Place the cumin seeds in a large frying pan over medium heat. Toast, shaking the pan often, until the cumin turns brown and fragrant, about 5 minutes. Turn off the heat and transfer the seeds to a large plate to cool. Once cool, grind in a spice grinder to a fine powder. Store in an airtight container in a cool, dark, dry spot for up to 4 months.

Tomato-Onion-Peanut Chutney

Tomato chutney always finds a home on my table. This version is a little different because of the peanuts, which add a wonderful texture.

⅓ cup/160 ml canola or grapeseed oil

36 fresh or 54 frozen curry leaves, roughly torn

12 dried red chiles

2 tsp brown mustard seeds

2 tsp cumin seeds

½ tsp ground turmeric

2 medium red onions, halved and thinly sliced

1 cup/145 g raw, skinned peanuts

3½ lb/1.6 kg tomatoes, roughly chopped

9 oz/255 g tomato paste (or one 4.4-oz/125-g tube double-concentrated tomato paste)

2 tbsp sugar

1 tsp Sambhaar Powder (page 219) or curry powder

½ tsp cayenne pepper

1½ tbsp kosher salt, plus more if needed

Heat the canola oil with the curry leaves, chiles, mustard seeds, and cumin seeds in a large frying pan over medium-high heat until the cumin is golden and fragrant, about 2 minutes. Stir in the turmeric and cook until the chiles darken, 1 to 2 minutes longer. Stir in the onions and cook until they have wilted and are opaque, 5 to 7 minutes. Stir in the peanuts, cook for 3 minutes, and then add the tomatoes, tomato paste, sugar, sambhaar powder, cayenne, and salt. Cook for 10 minutes, stirring often, pressing the tomatoes up against the sides of the pot to crush them.

Reduce the heat to medium and cook until the tomato juices are reduced and the chutney is thick and jammy, stirring often, 20 to 35 minutes (in the summer when tomatoes are juicy, it may take longer to thicken; in the winter, it may happen more quickly). Taste, adding more salt if needed, and then transfer to an airtight container and refrigerate for up to 1 week. Makes about 6 cups/1.4 L.

FARMHOUSE RESOURCES

Living on a farm is wonderful and charming, and also requires a lot of conducting and orchestration of little details to make everything seem seamless. Some of these details require our pantry to be stocked with all kinds of items, from foreign and exotic to local and artisanal. It's also imperative that our home has a stockpile of kitchen equipment and basics to keep the kitchen prepared for any need and occasion.

Farm life teaches us about investing our money wisely. We buy quality items that will last us a long time. If we buy cookware, we buy items that will last longer than our lifetime. Ditto for bakeware and knives. When we buy spices, we buy them whole and grind them as needed. As people who live on a farm, we also pay attention to what we buy, how we buy it, where we buy it, and how and when it comes to us. All of this helps us remain more connected to the earth and ensures that we make the smartest buying decisions.

From the choices we make for our cleaning supplies to the ones we make when buying kitchenware and foods, each decision impacts our lives and those who follow us. With this in mind, we share here an indispensable list of the people, places, and companies—local and farther afield—that make our life in Washington County more delicious by their hard work and passionate endeavors.

3-Corner Field Farm
Beautiful sheep's milk cheeses, yogurt, lamb yarn, and soap are made by Karen at her Shushan, New York, farm. Their *brebis blanche* and feta are often found on our brunch table.
www.dairysheepfarm.com

A&J Enterprises
Our one-stop shop for nearly all things farm related, from work books to garden supplies and livestock feed.
www.a-jenterprises.com

Agricultural Stewardship Association
ASA is a community-supported land trust dedicated to protecting local farmland from encroaching development.
www.agstewardship.org

Allen Brothers
When Charlie and I are in the mood to splurge on the finest-quality prime and Wagyu Kobe-style beef, tiger shrimp, and lobster tails, we look no further than Allen Brothers. From humanely raised veal to the most luscious dry-aged steakhouse-style steaks and delicious prepared foods (like my lamb burgers), Chicago-based Allen Brothers offers an entire catalog of superior-quality foods.
www.allenbrothers.com

American Livestock Breeds Conservancy

Dedicated to protecting rare breeds and conserving genetic diversity in American livestock, this conservancy is our source for choosing animal breeds to populate the farm.
www.albc-usa.org

American Masala Farm

Read all about our farm and its history, the history of Hebron, New York, and view photos of our heritage-breed chickens, ducks, guinea hens, goose eggs, hand-raised chevon (baby goats), and lambs on our Web site.
www.americanmasalafarm.com

Aunt Sally's Catering

Sally Longo is the host of *Dinner at 8* on local channel 8, and going anywhere with her is like walking with a major celebrity at your side. Her food is a mirror image of the times we live in—worldly, diverse, delicious.
www.adkcookbook.com

Battenkill Kitchen

This shared-use nonprofit kitchen is devoted to educating adults and youths. The Battenkill Kitchen provides seminars and cooking classes on mindful and healthful cooking and global flavors, as well as an eight-hundred-square-foot commercial food production facility for rent to local residents and food start-ups.
www.battenkillkitchen.org

Battenkill Valley Creamery

Award-winning Holstein and Jersey cow's milk are the specialties at Battenkill Valley Creamery, available from the farm or from select retailers.
www.battenkillcreamery.com

Black Lab Farm

Brian and Christina farm their land in Greenwich, New York, with great attention and produce an incredible array of black raspberries, Chandler blueberries, supersweet strawberries, and some of the best vegetables around.
(518) 744-9174

Byrd Mill Company

Peanut flour adds a beautifully nutty flavor to the coating for my fried chicken. It's also excellent in tart crusts for a peanuty essence. Based in peanut-centric Virginia, Byrd Mill has been milling flour for centuries.
www.byrdmill.com

Caldrea

This company is one of our favorites for Earth-friendly, animal-friendly home-keeping aids.
www.caldrea.com

California Olive Ranch

This ranch features first-class award-winning olive oils from the Northern California foothills.
www.californiaoliveranch.com

Chaiwalla

Mary O'Brien's all-too-charming teahouse in Salisbury, Connecticut, offers beautiful tea and tomato tarts, as well as wicked-good desserts.
(860) 435-9758

Chickens

There are a few sources we turn to for buying chicks. Here are our favorites.

Meyer Hatchery
www.meyerhatchery.com

Murray McMurray Hatchery
www.mcmurrayhatchery.com

Stromberg's Chicks and Gamebirds
www.strombergschickens.com

The Chocolate Mill Pastry Shop and Café

Glens Falls, New York, is said to be having a renaissance, and the proof is in the pudding—or *crème pâtissier*—made by Certified Master Pastry Chef Frank Vollkommer and his wife, Jessica. The perfect mix of talent and kindness, the couple creates food that captivates anyone with a sweet tooth.
www.chocolatemillcafe.com

Comollo Antiques and Fine Wine

This is our spendy destination for fabulous wine and antiques in the Green Mountains.
www.vtantiques.com

Consider Bardwell Farm

Award-winning European-style goat's milk and cow's milk cheeses come from Angela Miller's farm in West Pawlet, Vermont. We won't list the cheeses we like—because we love them all. It's a great place to stop by, visit the goats, talk to the überfriendly cheesemaking team, and enjoy a "Pawletty" at the café. Real artisanal cheese devotees should definitely check out the cheesemaking classes.
www.considerbardwellfarm.com

Country Gallery Antiques

Beautiful Scandinavian antiques abound at Country Gallery Antiques in Rupert, Vermont. The selection of rag rugs, antique cookery gadgets, country farm tables, and grandfather clocks is mind blowing.
www.country-gallery.com

Courthouse Community Center

Offering performing arts, crafts, and educational activities for the people of Washington County, this community center is also the location of the Courthouse Community Garden, whose goal is to educate the youth of Salem, New York, about how to grow, process, and market food.
www.salemcourthouse.org

Cuisinart

I rely on my Cuisinart food processor to make quick work of chopping and shredding vegetables, emulsifying mayonnaise, and even making pizza dough. The Cuisinart ice-cream machine is a luxury that creates the silkiest, easiest homemade ice creams.
www.cuisinart.com

Culinary Institute of America (CIA)

The nation's premier culinary academy—with locations in New York, California, Texas, and Singapore—CIA offers professional degrees and seminars and programs for recreational cooks.
www.ciachef.edu

Dancing Ewe Farm
Delicious sheep's milk ricotta, pecorino, and caciotta made by Jody and Luisa Somers have become staples in our refrigerator.
www.dancingewe.com

De Gustibus Cooking School
This cooking school on the top floor of Macy's in Herald Square has been a New York City institution since 1980. It was recently bought by Sal Rizzo (see his recipe for Scrambled Eggs with Tomatoes, Onions, and Herbs, page 75), who is maintaining tradition by showcasing new and emerging chefs and cookbook authors, as well as the names we all know. I frequently teach classes here when in New York.
www.degustibusnyc.com

Emile Henry
An exquisite collection of enameled stoneware and tableware that goes from oven to table in high style can be found at Emile Henry. I am a huge fan of everything they do, from dinner plates to ramekins, tagines, braisers, and pie plates.
www.emilehenry.com

Falk Culinair
This beautiful brushed copper cookware comes from Belgium. We use their massive 13½-qt/ 12.7-L pot for making jam.
www.copperpans.com

Flying Pigs Farm
Heritage breed pork from the Battenkill River Valley is what you'll find at this farm.
www.flyingpigsfarm.com

Foods of India
The absolute freshest spices, legumes, and hard-to-find Indian ingredients can be found here.
(212) 683-4419, 121 Lexington Avenue, New York, New York

Gardenworks
Our local source in Salem, New York, for incredible blueberries and raspberries, as well as cheeses, flowers, organic salad greens, herbs, and pumpkins in the fall and winter.
www.gardenworksfarm.com

Granite•Ware
We love our go-to speckled cookware for canning and preserving.
www.columbianhp.com

Hicks Orchard
This is New York state's oldest u-pick orchard. We love the sour cherries, summer plums, pumpkins, and goats.
www.hicksorchard.com

The Hyde Collection
Though we are a four-hour drive from the galleries and art museums of New York City, we get our art fix at this gem in Glens Falls that offers a rare opportunity to view art *en salon*. The 2,800-piece collection offers seasonal installations from Degas to Wyeth.
www.hydecollection.org

Illy
Days begin early at the farm, and for Charlie and many of our guests, that means fresh-brewed Illy coffee first thing.
www.illyusa.com

J.K. Adams

Located in the handsome village of Dorset, Vermont, J.K. Adams has been bringing New England craftsmanship to the industry for more than sixty-five years. It's a great source for beautiful cutting boards, wine racks, bowls, and more. www.jkadams.com

Kaiser Bakeware

I'm a big fan of their new state-of-the-art La Forme Plus collection. www.kaiserbakeware.com

Kerrygold

There is something to be said for good butter—it not only tastes better, it performs better, too. Kerrygold is our favorite widely available variety. www.kerrygold.com

King Arthur Flour

This brand is our choice for pure and consistently performing flour, grains, and baking notions. www.kingarthurflour.com

KitchenAid

We'd be lost without KitchenAid's stand mixer, food processor, and immersion blender, not to mention its line of professional-quality kitchen accessories. www.kitchenaid.com

Korin

Korin is known around the world for the best-quality knives and also for a beautiful collection of tableware, top-notch kitchenware, and superb spices and sauces, like *shichimi* and aged shoyu (Japanese soy sauce). For many years, Korin was the well-kept secret of the world's top chefs—it's now open to the public! www.korin.com

The Lawyer and the Baker

We often plan a trip to Manchester Center, Vermont, just to visit this lovely café. The egg salad is incredible—and I have been known to buy an entire sheet pan of their incredible pecan squares or a whole tart or pie. **(802) 366-8018, 32 Bonnet Street, Manchester Center, Vermont**

LeCreuset

We love these traditional enameled cast-iron pots (and our favorite silicone spatula) for making dal and rice, and for braising. www.lecreuset.co.uk

Locust Grove Smokehouse

Our local Argyle, New York–based butcher is who we turn to for specialty hard-to-find cuts and last-minute requests. www.locustgrovesmokehouse.com

Lodge Cast Iron

My cast-iron skillet is always on my stove top. I find it indispensable for making biscuits, cornbread, upside-down cakes, and steaks. www.lodgemfg.com

Lucini Italia
Prepared in small batches and using 100 percent natural ingredients, Lucini's olive oils,
vinegars, Parmigiano-Reggiano cheese, and
tomato products are bar none.
www.lucini.com

Mauviel
I love the look of copper pans hanging from
the pot rack in my kitchen. Mauviel's French
imports are as functional as they are beautiful.
www.mauvielusa.com

**Mrs. London's Bakery and Café and
Max London's Restaurant**
A trip to Saratoga Springs is always a treat because
we get to purchase the incredible croissants,
cannelés, and other delectable creations (many
made with eggs from our farm) of Wendy and
Michael London at Mrs. London's Bakery. Max,
their son, is showing the world his own brilliant
culinary talents in the restaurant next door.
www.mrslondons.com
www.maxlondons.com

Mrs. Meyer's Clean Day
We love the lemon verbena dishwasher gel—
it's the bees' knees for superior scrubbing.
www.mrsmeyers.com

National Peanut Board
The National Peanut Board is an organization
dedicated to supporting American peanut
farmers. Its Web site provides information
about peanut farmers, gluten-free cooking,
and nutrition facts about this popular legume.
www.nationalpeanutboard.org

Nielsen-Massey Vanillas
This is our go-to source for reliable, superb-
quality, origin-specific vanilla bean, vanilla
paste (an addiction of mine), and extracts, as
well as other flavorings.
www.nielsenmassey.com

Rancho Gordo
This ranch produces incredibly beautiful
heirloom dried beans.
www.ranchogordo.com

Republic of Beans
Discover chef Cesare Casella's noble pursuit to
bring dried Italian heirloom beans, lentils, and
rice to the plates of Americans.
www.republicofbeans.com

Royal Oak Peanuts
Big, fat, crunchy, and delicious, these are hands-
down our favorite Virginia-grown peanuts.
They're roasted to order in peanut oil for the
freshest flavor.
www.royaloakpeanuts.com

Saratoga Apple
If there is an apple on our counter, it more than
likely came from either our tree or Saratoga
Apple. We come here for our favorite heirloom
apples, like Belle de Boskoop, Fortunes, and
Northern Spys, as well as plums, black currants,
and chestnuts.
www.saratogaapple.com

Seventh Generation
This Burlington, Vermont–based and Earth-friendly company is a producer of household cleaners and recycled paper products.
www.seventhgeneration.com

Sheldon Farms
Pat and Albert Sheldon's family farm in Salem is famous for its Butter and Sugar sweet corn and many varieties of potatoes, as well as other seasonal veggies. They also bottle their own maple syrup.
www.sheldonfarmsny.com

SieMatic
The finest German engineering for the home kitchen begins with SieMatic. The lentil storage alone is worth the price!
www.siematic.com

Slack Hollow Farm
Our kitchen often features organic herbs and greens from Seth Jacobs, one of the nation's pioneers in organic farming.
www.slackhollowfarm.com

Slow Food
This nonprofit foundation was founded to counteract fast food, fast life, and the disappearance of local food traditions.
www.slowfoodusa.org

Someday Farm
Scout and her family have been farming her grandfather's Dorset, Vermont, land organically for decades. The quality and care is noticed by all who buy their fruits, vegetables, chickens, and maple syrup.
(802) 362-0165

Summerfield Farm
Organic Katahdin lamb from the valleys and hills of Washington County is offered at Summerfield Farm.
(518) 642-0150

Timeless Natural Food
Timeless Natural Food produces high-quality certified-organic cereal grains, pulse crops, and edible seeds from the Golden Triangle, Montana's most productive agricultural area.
www.timelessfood.com

Ultramarinos
Chef Maricel Presilla's Latin specialty store sells hard-to-find ingredients like frozen tamarillos, a multitude of chiles, and chocolate from Venezuela.
www.ultramarinos.biz

Vermont Butter and Cheese Creamery
Allison, Bob, and their team make us (and our guests) smile daily with their rich and creamy crème fraîche (the house staple when we don't have our own in the fridge) and cultured butter with sea salt crystals.
www.vermontcreamery.com

Vermont Country Store
At this idyllic country store, you can sample local cheese and fudge, try on clothes, swing in the hammocks, or find a rarified perfume, shampoo, or potion from yesteryear.
www.vermontcountrystore.com

Vermont Soapstone
Glenn Bowman and his team know soapstone. Outstanding quality, great design—the best stone for kitchens!
www.vermontsoapstone.com

Viking
Viking makes infallible and aesthetically stunning ranges, wine cabinetry, refrigerators, and dishwashers.
www.vikingrange.com

Vitamix
Buy one now, seriously. Yes, it costs more than any other blender, but this is a workhorse that you can pass down to the grandchildren.
www.vitamix.com

Wade Ceramics
Wade Ceramics produces high-quality earthenware and porcelain products, as well as the American Masala line of servingware and cookware.
www.wade.co.uk

Wilson Homestead Old Books and Antiques—and Hearth Cooking
Vintage cookware, dinnerware, cookbooks, and fun conversation with Sally and Joe, our neighbors, can all be had at their business, the Wilson Homestead. Mid-winter through early spring, Sally offers hearth cooking classes that bring participants back to an era of homesteader cooking over an open fire.
(518) 854-3134

Windy River Farm
For grass-raised beef from Shushan, New York, go no farther than Windy River Farm.
(518) 339-5059

INDEX